I0816042

Crucial Commitments

A Tyndale nonfiction imprint

Crucial Commitments

5 Simple Decisions That Members of Healthy and Growing Churches Make

Thom S. Rainer

Visit Tyndale online at tyndale.com.

Visit Tyndale Momentum online at tyndalemomentum.com.

Crucial Commitments: Five Simple Decisions That Members of Healthy and Growing Churches Make

Cover design by Faceout Studio, Tim Green

Interior design by Brandi Davis

The author is represented by Alive Literary Agency, www.aliveliterary.com.

Some names and details have been modified for the privacy of the churches or individuals involved.

For information about special discounts for bulk purchases, please contact Tyndale House Publishers at csresponse@tyndale.com, or call 1-855-277-9400.

Library of Congress Cataloging-in-Publication Data

A catalog record for this book is available from the Library of Congress.

Printed in China

32 31 30 29 28 27 26
7 6 5 4 3 2 1

To

Harper Rainer,

my granddaughter, filled with laughter and joy.

It's contagious.

And always to

Nellie Jo.

You love me with grace—

unmerited, undeserved, and amazing.

Contents

Introduction

Going to Church Without Going Anywhere

I had never made a call like this one.

And I have to admit I almost backed out several times.

Lucas and Ava were getting married in five months. At the time, I was a pastor in St. Petersburg, Florida. Though I didn't offer marriage counseling myself, I required all couples to receive premarital counseling before they could be married in the church. I gave them a list of seven church-approved counselors in the community so they could choose one.

But I kept putting off the recommendation. I knew why I was hesitating this time: I lacked the courage to make the call.

You see, two days earlier, Lucas had stopped by my office just to chat. He didn't have an agenda—he was an extrovert who loved talking about almost anything, especially college football, which happens to be my favorite sport as well. Even better, we both cheered for the same college team.

Though I'm an introvert, I find conversations about college football energizing. Before I knew it, we had talked for forty-five minutes. I finally had to end our discussion, so I made a transition statement: "Lucas, I know you're excited about this upcoming wedding."

That's when he said it. His comment sounded offhand, but it took my breath away.

"I guess so, but if it doesn't work out, we're not locked into anything."

Did I hear him correctly? Did he just suggest marriage was no big deal? Was he putting divorce on the table before even saying his vows? And did Ava know he felt this way?

I asked him to clarify. Yes, I had heard him right. Marriage, to Lucas, was just another phase of life. He genuinely didn't expect his first marriage to be his last. He was preparing to get married without a full commitment to marriage. I should have confronted him more boldly before he walked away.

Shame on me.

From One Marriage to Another

Many years passed. This time, I was in a conversation with a woman named Jane. I was much older by then—hopefully wiser too. I was no longer serving as a pastor; my new role was dean of a seminary.

I was speaking at a conference about the importance of the local church and the priority of committed church membership. During a break, Jane asked if she could speak with me. She told me she respected my commitment to the local church, but her own views were different. I remember her exact words: "Jesus and I get along just fine by ourselves. We don't need others."

In other words, she felt it was legalistic to expect people to go to church.

Calling Lucas

Let me return to that dreaded call I eventually made to Lucas. I told him I would be honored to perform his wedding to Ava. But first we had to address his "contingency plan" for if things didn't work out. Lucas was furious.

"There's nothing wrong with being prepared for a divorce," he insisted. "Especially since half of all marriages fail."

I knew those numbers were inflated, but I also knew that it wouldn't help to debate the issue.

I wish I could say the story ended well. It didn't. Lucas's anger escalated to profanity. Both he and Ava left the church. They held their wedding at a beautiful outdoor venue, with someone else performing the ceremony.

Their marriage lasted four years.

I can assure you, I took no satisfaction in being right.

Marriage to Each Other and Marriage to the Bride of Christ

Marriage is a sacred institution that God established from the very beginning. Genesis 2:24 establishes that "a man leaves his father and mother and is joined to his wife, and the two are united into one." This verse underscores the divine design for human marriage—a bond of unity, love, and commitment that reflects God's own faithful character.

In marriage, husbands and wives are called to mirror the profound love Christ has for his church. As Paul explains in Ephesians 5:25-26, "Husbands, this means love your wives, just as Christ loved the church. He gave up his life for her to make her holy and clean." That sacrificial love elevates marriage from a mere social contract to a living symbol of God's care and redemption.

Likewise, the marriage between Christ and his church is depicted as the ultimate celebration of love and commitment. Revelation 19:7 joyfully proclaims, "Let us be glad and rejoice. . . . For the time has come for the wedding feast of the Lamb, and his bride has prepared herself." Here, the church is portrayed as a radiant bride, lovingly prepared for union with her groom—a union marked by purity, dedication, and everlasting love.

In both human marriage and the spiritual union between Christ and the church, God reveals his deep desire for covenant relationships. We are called to embrace selfless love, intentional commitment, and a heartfelt dedication to reflect God's grace in every aspect of our lives.

And Then There Was Jane

There is more than a nuanced difference between my two stories. Lucas clearly rejected any long-term commitment to Ava. In fact, he believed the odds were stacked against their marriage—or any marriage—and felt he needed an escape clause. He left a back door open and eventually walked out.

Jane, on the other hand, sincerely believed she was committed to the church. Her definition of *church*, however, did not include gathering, worshiping together, or serving other members. It was more about her own experience—of being taught and feeling inspired. Preferably in the privacy of her own home. Sadly, Jane's understanding of church life is increasingly common today. She "goes to church" without going anywhere.

But a local church that doesn't gather is not a genuine community. It does not reflect a committed relationship with Jesus, who declared that he would build a church that the powers of hell could not conquer (Matthew 16:18). We cannot go to church without going somewhere.

In the New Testament, the church is a congregation of people who make some crucial commitments—to the Lord and to each other. Those commitments are the foundation for this book, and they reflect the truths of Scripture.

Being a part of Christ's church is not a solo endeavor. It is a vital connection to other committed believers, as together we follow our Savior and Lord.

Indeed, like any good marriage, the local church needs radical commitments to survive, much less thrive. It's simple, but it's not simplistic.

Let's find out why.

Part 1

The *Why* of Church Membership

The death of my grandson Will was not unexpected. But we had only a short time to prepare for it.

A few days before Will's birth, my daughter-in-law Rachel began noticing some problems with her pregnancy. To this point, everything had gone well, and the baby was close to full term.

An initial call to her doctor relieved some of her immediate anxiety. He thought the problems were not serious, but he still wanted to see her.

But the problems were indeed serious, and the diagnosis was heart-shattering. Will had a condition that would almost certainly be fatal. The doctor said he would probably not live long after birth. Sadly, both diagnoses were accurate. After Rachel gave birth to her son, he lived exactly one hour as she and my son Jess held him close.

In many ways, though, the story was just beginning.

Jess and Rachel had been committed church members from the earliest days of their marriage. They loved doing for others. They loved serving others. In every church they'd been a part of, they were primarily known for giving and serving.

I remember a conversation I had with one of their former pastors. He laughed as he told me he had become hesitant to ask Jess and Rachel to help in any new ministry areas, because they always said yes.

"But you never got the impression they were serving out of guilt or obligation," he added with a smile. "They found *joy* in giving and serving."

This time, however, the roles were reversed. They were on the receiving end of the giving, serving, and doing. I watched with amazement as the body of Christ ministered to my son and daughter-in-law. I stood in awe as their fellow church members took care of every known need Jess and Rachel had—servanthood that continued unabated for weeks after Will's death. I saw the body of Christ come together to bear the burden of others the way God intended.

I was in deep pain for my youngest son and his wife, and I grieved the loss of my grandson. But every day when I left the hospital—or later, Jess and Rachel's home—I felt incredible comfort knowing they were in good hands. The church cared for them, loved them, and served them. I witnessed firsthand what it means to find purpose and meaning together in the local church. I saw clearly why God never intended for us to be solo Christians.

That local congregation was truly a caring body, functioning as the hands and feet of our Savior.

Significance and Purpose

Here is the central theme of this book: *Your best hope for finding significance and purpose in life is through your local church.* Members who live out that purpose in their local church will lead a transformation in the congregation.

I imagine that simple statement will evoke a variety of responses.

You may be nodding in agreement because you have discovered incredible joy and fulfillment in your church. You're not looking for something more; you've already found it in a church in your community. You can't imagine life without your church. Indeed, you can't imagine finding meaning and purpose apart from your church.

Or maybe you're not so sure. You're a member of a church and you attend somewhat regularly, but while you see good things in your church, you also see some things that aren't so good. It seems like a stretch to claim that a life of significance and purpose is found largely in the context of the local church.

Or maybe you were once consistent in church attendance, but not anymore. Perhaps the COVID-19 pandemic showed you a life outside the local church that *seemed manageable—maybe even comfortable*. You've started wondering, *Do I really need to get up on Sunday morning and go to church? Do I need to go every week? What's wrong with attending in person occasionally and watching online the rest of the time?*

Maybe you're skeptical. You're not convinced the local church is all that important. You've seen the ugly side, and you think that people outside the church often behave better than those inside it. Perhaps the idea that the local church could be the primary place to find significance and meaning strikes you as absurd. At best, you see it as just another cultural institution that is losing relevance. Maybe you're questioning whether you want to be part of a local congregation at all.

I understand. I've heard the full spectrum of responses. More and more people today are questioning the value of the local church in their lives.

But there's a reason God established the local church as his plan A for reaching the world with the good news of the gospel. And there's a reason he didn't give us a plan B.

Let's take a look.

1

Imagine That

Imagine for a moment that churches around the world truly made a difference. Imagine walking into a church and being accepted and embraced just as you are. Imagine that you could change the world through your local church. Imagine your life's purpose being fulfilled in the context of your local church.

If it's tough for you to conceive of such a scenario, would you consider a few examples of people whose lives have truly been transformed through their churches? If you'll bear with me, I'll share some stories about the life-changing power of the local church—stories I've heard directly from members.

Helping the Hurting

Westbend Church is one of thousands of congregations that meet near a beach or waterway in Florida. Indeed, the sun, sand, and surf attract millions of tourists every year. Add the favorable tax structure in Florida that draws a continual influx of retirees, and you can understand the state's appeal.

Yet the same beautiful bodies of water that draw the tourists and retirees are also pathways for illegal drug trafficking. The fentanyl trade is one of the deadliest and fastest growing illegal industries in south Florida. Fentanyl takes lives. Fentanyl overdoses challenge the medical system. Fentanyl trafficking changes tourist havens into areas to be avoided. And fentanyl destroys families.

Westbend Church has hosted countless funerals for victims of fentanyl. Members and leaders noticed a heartbreaking pattern at these funerals: The deceased were often young parents, leaving behind young children.

Madeline, a member of the church for twenty-seven years, explained, "I was part of the group at our church that started asking questions about these children. We wondered what their home life was like, especially if a parent was using fentanyl. And sadly, we guessed right: Many of these kids had a surviving parent who was not able to care for them."

With so many children in need and few foster homes available, the local child services system was overwhelmed. So a group of Westbend members began taking foster kids into their homes. And because reunification of original families is not always possible, Westbend also became a place where many children were adopted.

Neither fostering nor adoption is easy. It's often quite challenging. Still, members of Westbend Church felt compelled to act. They believed this was the path Jesus would have them follow.

"Jesus had an obvious affection for children," Madeline said. "We decided as a church that we could do more together than alone. We created a fostering network so we could help each other when someone needed a break. We started a prayer ministry—for the children, for their families, and for us as foster parents."

Westbend has now been a hub of fostering activity for twelve years. "And we can see the fruit," Madeline said. "We see changed lives. We see lives that have been saved. We have made a positive impact to counteract the fentanyl problem in our community. We set out to bless our town, but the blessing we've *received* has been far greater."

Imagine being part of a church whose ministry is used by God to make a tangible difference in the surrounding community. Imagine how your sense of purpose would be renewed. Imagine being part of a church where your life is marked by profound significance.

The Power of Prayer for Families

Deerfield Community Church is located in the heart of an unincorporated community of 8,000 residents in central Indiana. A high school physics teacher named Daniel first noticed an unsettling trend: More and more of his students were coming from single-parent homes. Several parents of kids in his classes had divorced within the past two years. He was concerned.

A demographic study confirmed Daniel's observations. Divorces were on the rise, families were breaking apart, and the children were paying the price.

Daniel set up an appointment with his pastor, Bryan, who had been part of the Deerfield community and church for nine years. Bryan encouraged church members to bring ideas and solutions whenever they shared concerns, so Daniel knew he had to be prepared to discuss more than just a list of problems. So he suggested a simple but potentially powerful ministry: praying for families in the community.

"I've been seeing more struggling families and divorces the past few years than at any other time," Daniel told Bryan. "I did some research, and our divorce rate has almost doubled in five years. We're in a crisis."

Daniel outlined a plan with four major components:

1. A monthly prayer ministry, involving fifteen church members at a time. Each member would commit to

one month of praying for ten homes. Over a year, that would cover all 1,800 homes in Deerfield.

2. A brief, handwritten follow-up note to each home, letting them know they were being prayed for and providing contact information for prayer requests.
3. A dedicated prayer team to respond to any requests that came in. As the ministry grew, they expanded this team to five people.
4. A connecting ministry. When someone visited the church because of the prayer outreach, leaders paired them with a church member or family who would invite them to lunch. Many of the guests accepted this invitation.

Daniel's excitement was palpable when he described the results. "We started by simply observing the rising divorce rate. Now we're part of a ministry to families, sharing the gospel and connecting them to resources such as marriage counseling. My own life has become so much richer through this ministry."

Imagine being part of a church that God uses to rescue marriages, share the gospel, and serve as a powerful conduit for prayer. Imagine discovering that your life has a purpose you never knew was possible. Imagine seeing entire families transformed—often right before your eyes.

Second Responders for Jesus

A tornado left massive damage in an Oklahoma community. Two lives were lost, and it could have been far worse. Most people had found shelter in time.

Still, the destruction was staggering.

That was ten years ago, and Marge and Ben remembered it vividly.

"I remember walking outside after the tornado passed," Marge said. "*Our* home was fine, but within a quarter-mile radius, the damage was overwhelming."

Ben recalled, "We were just two people, and we weren't sure what we could do. While we were walking around, listening to the sirens of the first responders, I got a call from a friend at our church, the Church of Hope, who was also on the city council. He told me the high school was severely damaged, and he'd heard that the city wouldn't have enough capacity to house all the displaced people. Since I was an elder, he asked me to contact the others to see if we could open the church as a shelter."

The elders agreed immediately. Church members began securing cots, baby beds, clothes, toys, and toiletries. One group was responsible for meals and water. Three church members who were insurance agents worked to get adjusters out quickly.

"I've never seen our church mobilize like that," Marge said. "The response didn't slow down for days. Some of the men went door to door with chain saws to clear toppled trees. Others worked with roofers to get tarps on salvageable homes. I started calling it a 'second responder' ministry. One of our members, Carlos, put up a sign: Second Responder Ministry of the Church of Hope."

Within a few days, the immediate crisis ended, and most people had found a place to stay. Marge wrote down everything she could remember about their response efforts.

"Though I hoped we wouldn't need it again," she said, "I wanted us to be ready."

Two weeks later, another tornado hit a town ninety minutes away. When a pastor there asked the Church of Hope for help, the leaders mobilized a response within two hours, sending a team to help the other church respond more effectively.

"It's now been a decade," Ben said, "and the Second Responder ministry is still flourishing. Sometimes we partner with other Christian relief organizations; sometimes it's just us."

"I've been the hands and feet of Christ in tornadoes, hurricanes, floods, and mudslides," Marge added. Our whole church caught this vision. We're on mission almost every month. My life has incredible purpose now. Many of us say the same thing: We couldn't do this alone. We do it as the body of Christ."

"I never could have imagined my life would be so rich," Ben said with a smile.

Imagine being connected to a church that truly becomes the hands and feet of Christ. Imagine changing the world one disaster response at a time.

Powerful Sermons in a Powerful Church

It began with a conversation between Debra and her sister-in-law, Phoebe.

"I was getting tired of Phoebe telling me how much she was growing spiritually under her pastor's preaching," Debra admitted. "I decided to watch one of his sermons online. It was okay—nothing great."

The next day, when Phoebe predictably brought up the sermon again, Debra told her it wasn't that special.

"She just said, 'Of course not. You didn't get it.'"

Phoebe explained that she used to have the same attitude, but she started praying specifically for her own heart, asking God to speak to her through the sermons.

"It had never occurred to me to pray for myself regarding a pastor's preaching," Debra said. "But I was convicted and decided to try it."

Debra also shared the idea with a few friends. Before long, at least a hundred people in the church were praying that God would speak to them through the pastor's sermons. It felt like a movement was gathering steam.

"It's now common to see a lot of people taking notes during the sermon," Debra said. "There's a hunger for the Bible and a desire to hear from God, unlike anything I've ever seen."

After a month or two, Debra asked her pastor, Craig, how he felt about all the note-taking. He admitted he was confused at first—he didn't know what was going on or who to ask. When Debra explained her simple initiative, Craig began to cry.

"He told me he'd been dying a death of a thousand cuts from constant complaints. He'd even thought about leaving the ministry."

In the weeks that followed, Debra noticed a renewed energy in Pastor Craig. By every measure, the church was experiencing spiritual growth. Many described the worship services as "a time when God is doing a powerful and obvious work."

"It's a movement of God," Debra said. "I can't wait for worship each week. My life is being transformed by God's Word. And I know I'm not the only one. So many of us have discovered new purpose and meaning."

Can You Imagine?

Imagine a church with a powerful ministry to help the hurting—where members come together and see real transformation in people's lives. You notice your town is changing for the better as well. You wake up every morning with a sense of anticipation for what God will do. You see church members working together with focus and purpose.

Imagine that.

Imagine being part of a church that prays faithfully for the community. Many of the people who are prayed for are deeply touched. Some begin attending your church, and marriages and families are restored. You can't wait to serve in this ministry. You've found a life purpose you never dreamed possible. God is using your church in remarkable ways.

Imagine that.

Imagine you're on the front lines of disaster relief through your church. You've joined fellow members in responding to tornadoes, hurricanes, floods, and fires. Though the tragedies are heartbreaking, your life has taken on new meaning. You realize you couldn't do this alone. You're part of the body of Christ functioning as it should.

Imagine that.

Imagine the worship service at your church is a highlight in your week. You sense God's presence. You study your Bible more than ever before—and enjoy it. When the pastor preaches, you hear the Word of God in a fresh, powerful way. You're not alone—others are experiencing the same transformation. It's a movement of God that affects the entire congregation.

Imagine that.

Would you want to be part of a church with these qualities? Would you make it a priority if you could truly see transformation in your life?

Perhaps you're thinking there's no perfect church like that. I understand. But by the time you finish this book, I pray you will see your church in a different light. I hope you'll see that you really can find purpose and meaning through the ministry of a local congregation. In fact, I hope you will come to realize that you will never find lasting purpose and meaning without a joyful connection to a local church family.

Yes, it's a bold claim. But walk with me through the roadblocks and problems common to local churches. Then let's see how God intends for us to flourish—together.

A transformed and transformational life through the local church? A life of significance and purpose found in the local church?

Yes.

Imagine that.

Three Questions

1. What are some characteristics a healthy church should exhibit?
2. Do you think most church members see their local church as a place to find purpose and significance? Why or why not?
3. What are some common characteristics of the churches we highlighted in this chapter?

2

Finding Purpose and Significance . . . Together

I am grateful beyond measure that you are reading this book. I have prayed that God will use it to make a difference in many lives. I pray that God will use it to make a difference in *your* life.

If you have read any of my previous books, you know I love the local church. Some of my books have focused on what it means to be a church member. Others have focused on how a Christian can live a life *on mission* for God. This book has similar themes, but it's also different in that it ties our commitment to our local church to the meaning and purpose in our lives.

My thesis is simple: God intends for us to have rich and meaningful lives as we work and serve together through the local church. This is what transforms congregations.

I know some people who would balk at that last phrase—*as we work and serve together through the local church.* Some would contend that we can find a rich and meaningful life outside of a local congregation. Others might even argue that getting involved in church life can be detrimental to our spiritual and emotional health.

Believe me, I get it. I've been to more than one church business meeting.

Still, I have to disagree, respectfully, with those who believe that our ultimate meaning in life can be found apart from the local church. That isn't what the Bible says, for starters. If you believe the Bible, you have to at least acknowledge the importance of the local church. After all, it is central to almost all the teaching in the New Testament after the four Gospels. For example, look at these facts:

- The book of Acts records the beginning of the church in Jerusalem and traces the founding and growth of many other churches from Asia Minor to Greece to Rome. Acts accounts for 14 percent of the New Testament.
- The apostle Paul wrote nine books directly to local congregations (Romans, 1 Corinthians, 2 Corinthians, Galatians, Ephesians, Philippians, Colossians, 1 Thessalonians, 2 Thessalonians) and four books to local church leaders (1 Timothy,

2 Timothy, Titus, Philemon). These thirteen letters account for 28 percent of the New Testament.
- Some or most of the other epistles are directed to or tied to local churches (Hebrews, James, 1 Peter, 2 Peter, 1 John, 2 John, 3 John, Jude, Revelation).

It is beyond dispute that the local church is a key focus in the New Testament. As God inspired the authors to write their letters, he clearly established the profound importance of local congregations.

If the local church is important to God, it should be important to us, as well.

But, you may argue, so many churches are messed up. I understand. In fact, in chapter 4 I will be as transparent and open as I can be in addressing some of these negative issues. So hold that thought for now and give me an opportunity to respond. I simply ask that you maintain a level of openness as you read.

Obviously, I can't know every one of my readers personally. And I don't presume to know where you are in your relationship to a local church. But in my approach here, I'm trying to cast a wide net.

Maybe you're totally disconnected from a local congregation. Maybe you're not even a Christian. You might have picked up this book out of curiosity, or maybe someone encouraged you to read it. You may be doubtful or skeptical about my thesis. I'm just thankful you're here.

Maybe you're a Christian, but for reasons of your own you've never decided to join a church. Maybe you've been a member of one or more churches in your lifetime. Maybe you've slowly drifted from church involvement to the point where you are no longer connected at all. Maybe you've severed ties and left a church abruptly because you ran into the buzz saw of an abusive church member. Or you were belittled for suggesting some creative ideas. Or you discovered a power group that ran the church like their own fiefdom. Sadly, those are real issues in too many congregations.

Maybe you belong to a church, but like a lot of church members you don't participate as often as you once did. There was a time when people were at church two or three times a week. Now, for some, it's more like once or twice a month. Gathering with fellow believers is no longer the priority it once was. It's easier to sleep in, go to a sporting event, or spend time with the family after a long workweek. Church members who don't attend are in the process of slipping away from meaningful involvement.

You may find yourself in that "slipping away" category. You are finding fewer reasons to attend church and more reasons to do something else. Maybe you're asking yourself whether your commitment has truly been worth it. At times there has been pain and frustration in being part of a local congregation. You wonder whether God really wants you at your particular church.

Even the most active church members need occasional reminders of the importance of the local congregation. In far too many churches, leaders have low—even apologetic—expectations of their members. Some members need to be reminded that the work, ministry, service, and community of a local church have eternal and positive consequences. If we treat church membership like just another organization or civic club involvement, we will rightly question our commitment. We will wonder if we are wasting our time.

But let me say it again for emphasis: *God intends for us to have rich and meaningful lives as we work and serve together through the local church.* There is no other organization mentioned in the New Testament that carries the weight and importance of the local church. The church is that essential.

My premise may seem radical in light of the minimal commitment expectations in many local churches today. Still, the Bible is clear on the matter. If we really want to make a difference, if we're looking for something more, it will happen in the context of the local church. The apostle Paul wrote a lot to local churches—churches with diverse congregations, with different needs and different challenges. He wept for them. He longed to visit them. He prayed for them. He sought support for them. He encouraged them. He was willing to give his life for them.

Though not all of Paul's letters to the churches survived, God saw to it that the most important ones were preserved and handed down until they made it into the New Testament.

Of all the letters Paul wrote, the two that fascinate me the most are those we have to the Corinthians. You see, the Corinthian church was something of a problem child. A congregation founded on unity and service had become a church of divisiveness and self-centeredness. Those attitudes devolved into false teaching and immorality.

If you ever start to think that your church has problems, read 1 and 2 Corinthians. It's hard to even outline the two books because Paul addresses so many problems.

One thing that stands out when we read these two letters is that Paul mentions the name of the Lord again and again. He wanted to remind the church that they were no longer recognizing Jesus Christ as Lord. The worldliness of the city of Corinth was creeping into the church there. The members were all about putting themselves first. Serving had been replaced with self-serving, and disunity and arguments soon followed.

I mention these things as a simple reminder: You will never find a perfect church. Indeed, you will find many highly *imperfect* churches like the one in Corinth. But Paul never gave up on the local church. To the contrary, he exhorted and encouraged the members to make the church better.

How were the Corinthians to make their congregation better? Paul gives us an answer with two major themes.

Theme 1: Finding Meaning by Serving

One of the many problems in the Corinthian church was the misunderstanding and misuse of spiritual gifts. In 1 Corinthians 12:1, Paul tackles the issue head-on: "Dear brothers and sisters, regarding your question about the special abilities the Spirit gives us. I don't want you to misunderstand this."

But the Corinthians did indeed misunderstand the role of spiritual gifts. Many saw them as a means of establishing their own superiority. But Paul makes two points clear: Every Christian has a spiritual gift, and the Holy Spirit is the source of all of them (1 Corinthians 12:4, 7). If the same Holy Spirit is the source of every gift, no church member has bragging rights about any particular gift.

Then Paul makes it crystal clear that spiritual gifts have a singular purpose: "so we can help each other" (1 Corinthians 12:7).

Did you get that? When you became a Christian, the Holy Spirit empowered you with some very specific gifts and abilities. But those gifts have one purpose: *to help you serve others.*

Take a moment and imagine a church in which every member uses their spiritual gifts to serve others. Imagine a church where every member puts the needs of others before their own. Imagine a church where every member is concerned about others first.

If that hypothetical church existed, there would be no church fights. There would be no member disagreements. There would be no complaints—or if there were, they would be handled with grace and wisdom. See Acts 6:1-7 as an example.

Indeed, there would be *unity*. It would be a church that everyone, inside and out, would see as a testament to the great work of God.

We know the ideal, but we also know the reality: The perfect local church doesn't exist. And some are more imperfect than others.

In writing to the church at Corinth, Paul acknowledges the problems. He admonishes some of the greatest offenders. But he also encourages the church members to be part of the solution.

I am an imperfect leader. I have fallen short as a husband, a father, a granddad, a pastor, a CEO, and a friend. I could write a massive book on ways I have failed as a leader. (Or, as my wife would lovingly say, it would have to be a multivolume series.)

As a leader, I have used one response consistently with people who bring me complaints or problems. I say, "Okay, I understand the problem. Now tell me the solution." It's a reminder that anyone can see the negative, but we are supposed to be working together to make the situation better.

That is exactly what Paul tells the church at Corinth. He acknowledges the lack of perfection, the falling short of the ideal, but then he offers a vibrant metaphor to describe how church members can be part of the solution. He refers to the church as "the body of Christ" (1 Corinthians 12:12) and makes a simple but powerful point: Every part of the body is necessary. One part cannot function on its own without the others.

Paul begins by describing the human body: "The human body has many parts, but the many parts make up one whole body. So it is with the body of Christ" (1 Corinthians 12:12). He then refers to different parts of the human body: the foot, the hand, the ear, the eye, and the nose (implied through his reference to smell).

> Yes, the body has many different parts, not just one part. If the foot says, "I am not a part of the body because I am not a hand," that does not make it any less a part of the body. And if the ear says, "I am not part of the body because I am not an eye," would that make it any less a part of the body? If the whole body were an eye, how would you hear? Or if your whole body were an ear, how would you smell anything?
>
> But our bodies have many parts, and God has put each part just where he wants it."
>
> **1 CORINTHIANS 12:14-18**

Paul refers to the various parts as "members." As the members work together in unity and sacrifice, the entire body becomes stronger. "This makes for harmony among the members, so that all the members care for each other" (1 Corinthians 12:25).

Hardly a month goes by that I don't hear from someone who claims that the Bible says nothing about church membership. To the contrary, the passage above and others make a powerful case for church membership.

Granted, it's not like membership in a civic club or country club—where you pay your dues and get perks, privileges, and service in return. The local church is a communal organization in which members gladly give and joyfully seek to serve others. Committed membership, rightly and biblically practiced, is God's plan for the local church.

I'm sure you get the picture. God created us in his image to serve others. And he gave us the local church as the functioning organism through which our ongoing service happens.

So how do we find purpose and meaning in a local church that may come with a plethora of problems and dysfunctional members? We become part of the solution. We jump in and serve others, using the gifts the Holy Spirit has given us. We put others before ourselves. We become *members* of the body of Christ, fully functioning and serving others. And we seek to serve and to give, regardless of how others respond.

"But Thom," you say, "if you saw how messed up my

church is, you would never advocate that I throw myself into such an awful situation."

I understand what you're up against, and I never said it would be easy. We will look at the very real challenges of local churches in chapter 4. But first, Paul offers an overarching solution to our dilemma. He devotes an entire chapter to it in 1 Corinthians 13.

We often call it "the love chapter."

Theme 2: Finding Meaning by Practicing Biblical Love

I almost got tired of the love chapter.

In one year, I officiated more than thirty weddings. I was serving as pastor of a church that had, obviously, a lot of young people. My weekends were full of wedding rehearsals, rehearsal dinners, wedding ceremonies, and wedding receptions. And the wedding photos. I felt like the wedding photos would never end. Let's. Do. One. More. Photo.

I know. I didn't always have the best attitude. Shame on me. These were occasions of great celebration. They were joyous. And—to God be the glory—most of the marriages are still strong today.

But I admit I grew weary of the long weekends. The rehearsals. The rehearsal dinners. The receptions. Did I mention the wedding photos?

At one point, I grew weary of 1 Corinthians 13. Shame on me again.

It was the biblical passage of choice for many of the weddings. I guess I just wanted a bit more variety. I also questioned the use of the passage in a wedding ceremony since it is really about unity in the local church. It's about our relationship with other church members—not, I insisted at the time, about love between a husband and wife.

I hope I have grown beyond my theological nitpicking. I now realize that the passage can also be seen as a beautiful expression of love between a husband and a wife. Even though its original context was intended for church members relating to and serving one another, there is nothing wrong with reading the love chapter at a wedding.

But I still don't miss the wedding photos.

I know I am stating the obvious, but 1 Corinthians 13, the love chapter, follows 1 Corinthians 12, where Paul deals with the abuse of spiritual gifts in the church at Corinth. He instructs the church members on the purpose and function of spiritual gifts, and then reminds the church of the *why* of spiritual gifts. We serve the church and we serve those in the church because we love others as Christ loved us.

If we serve others with any motivation other than love, our service is in vain. The word that Paul uses for "love" in 1 Corinthians 13 is the Greek word *agape*, which is a love that is self-sacrificial, totally committed to the well-being of others, and unconditional. That is, it expects nothing in return.

In essence, it is the type of love perfectly demonstrated in Christ's sacrificial love for us. When you think about your relationships or potential relationships with other church members, keep this description of *agape* love in mind:

It is a love that is patient with other church members.

It is a love that is kind to other church members.

It is a love that is not jealous of other church members.

It is a love that is not boastful or proud toward other church members.

It is a love that is not rude to other church members.

It is a love that does not demand its own way from other church members.

It is a love that is not irritable with other church members.

It is a love that keeps no record of being wronged by other church members.

In 1 Corinthians 12, we learn about the *actions* of being church members. In 1 Corinthians 13, we learn about the *attitudes* of being church members. Simply stated, if we don't have an attitude of love, our actions are worthless. Paul sums it up well in 1 Corinthians 13:3: "If I gave everything I have to the poor and even sacrificed my body, I could boast about it; but if I didn't love others, I would have gained nothing."

We Are Family

The church is described a number of ways in the Bible. One of the metaphors is that of a family. When Paul wrote to the churches in Galatia, he addressed both doctrinal heresy and self-serving attitudes. Look at these profound words at the conclusion of his letter: "Let's not get tired of doing what is good. At just the right time we will reap a harvest of blessing if we don't give up. Therefore, whenever we have the opportunity, we should do good to everyone—especially to those in the family of faith" (Galatians 6:9-10).

Did you catch that? Paul encourages the Galatians to adopt a selfless attitude—to not grow weary of helping others. He reminds them that their blessing will come when they put others before themselves.

Notice who Paul says should be the recipients of this unconditional ministry. He refers to them as "the family of faith." He wants the members of the Galatian churches to think of one another as members of a family. It is a metaphor loaded with meaning.

What are the characteristics of a healthy family?

First, family members love each other unconditionally. They want the best for each other and are willing to do almost anything for the others' good. Perhaps the most poignant example comes from how parents care for their children. My wife and I raised three sons. We were not perfect parents, though my wife was a much better parent than I was. One particular example of her unconditional love comes to mind immediately.

We were at seminary and struggling financially. She and I did not exchange gifts with each other, so we could provide modest gifts for our sons on their birthdays and Christmas. One month, both our money and our food were almost gone. My wife would not let her three little boys go hungry, so she found a newspaper ad offering to buy plasma. She planned to go the next day and make that sacrifice.

God intervened in the afternoon mail with an unexpected check from my uncle. But Nellie Jo was fully prepared to do whatever it would take because of her unconditional love for her sons.

Unconditional love is the cornerstone of a healthy family.

Second, family members serve one another. Husbands serve their wives. Wives serve their husbands. Siblings serve siblings. Parents serve their children. And in their adult years, children serve their parents. Healthy familial bonds are strong. Serving comes naturally and joyfully. The gift of family is a call to the gift of service.

Third, families provide for one another. One of the first conflicts in the early church, which I alluded to earlier, occurred when the church stopped providing food for some of the widows. The situation described in Acts 6:1 is tense. Luke, the author, refers to "rumblings of discontent." The apostles made the bold move of tasking seven men with the assignment of taking care of the widows.

The church is a family. Like members of a healthy family, church members are to love one another. They are to serve one another. They are to provide for one another. The metaphor of family for the church is powerful. If there is a single characteristic of a healthy family, it is the trait of seeking to be last and putting other members before ourselves.

Pause for a moment and think about how you relate to other members of your church. Are you consistently looking out for their good? Are you putting your personal preferences aside for the betterment of others? Are you praying for them? Are you seeking ways to serve them?

I can hear the possible objections. "If you only knew some of the personalities in my church, you would understand why it's not easy to serve them. They are really difficult people."

I get it. In any group of relationships, there will be difficult people. That's why the metaphor of a family is so helpful. The Bible uses the word *member* to describe both those in a family and those in a church (Ephesians 2:19, 5:29-30). A member is part of something greater. Whether in a family or a church, members must put the greater good of the body before their own interests.

Paul made this point clear when he wrote to the factious church at Corinth that if any one member is not healthy, it hurts the entire body: "God has put the body together such that extra honor and care are given to those parts that have less dignity. This makes for harmony among the members, so that all the members care for each other. If one part suffers, all the parts suffer with it, and if one part is honored, all the parts are glad" (1 Corinthians 12:24-26).

Do you grasp the significance of these words? We are not merely to have membership in a church; we are to be members who put others first. It is in the context of community and caring that we learn each day to live more like Jesus. Church membership is not about perks and privileges. It is about learning the joy of caring for others in our congregational family.

Seeking Significance

Countless books and movies have been produced about the quest to find purpose and meaning in life. Millions of people follow countless paths on their search for significance. It is a never-ending journey. Christians, of course, know where to find meaning. We hear it directly from the words of Jesus in John 10:10: "The thief's purpose is to steal and kill and destroy. My purpose is to give them a rich and satisfying life." Jesus contrasts his mission with the mission of Satan.

One is a mission of life and meaning; the other is a mission of destruction and death.

Jesus had just told his listeners, "Yes, I am the gate. Those who come in through me will be saved" (John 10:9). He tells them he is the way of salvation. Indeed, he makes it clear he is the *only* way of salvation.

But Jesus doesn't end the story with the path of eternal salvation. He adds that he is also the way to finding meaning in our lives on earth. He is the path to an abundant life, a life that is rich and satisfying.

Still, many Christians ask *how*. How do we find the rich and satisfying life that Jesus promises? Where do we begin? The answer is right before our eyes in Scripture. We find our abundant life in Christ in the context of the local church. Simply stated, Christ intends for us to find meaning *together*, not alone.

I noted at the beginning of the chapter that the majority of the New Testament was written to, or about, local churches. It is powerfully clear that God intends for us to find the abundant life in the community we call church. In fact, Paul clearly states that the body of Christ today *is* the church: "All of you together are Christ's body, and each of you is a part of it" (1 Corinthians 12:27). Those words were written to the local church in Corinth. They carry the same meaning for our local churches today.

To say that meaning in life is found in Christ through the

local church is not a popular message in our culture today. Indeed, it is not always a popular message among *Christians*. Many insist that abundant life can or should be found independent of the body of Christ, the church.

But that is not what the Bible tells us. Meaning in life is found in Christ through his church.

That is where we find fellowship.

That is where we find accountability.

That is where we serve one another.

That is where discipleship takes place.

That is where our commitment is clear and evident.

Do you want to have a life that makes a difference? Do you desire a life deep in meaning, one that is rich and satisfying? Do you want to discover Christ's abundant life for you? Are you willing to make some radical commitments?

God intends for us to have a rich and meaningful life as we work and serve together. This life takes place in a community called the church. From the first church in Jerusalem to our churches today, Christians have lived out God's purpose and mission for their lives *together*, not alone. They have responded to the five crucial commitments we will examine in the second part of this book.

The objections to this path of meaning and fulfillment come not only from nonbelievers, but from believers as well. Some Christians don't buy into the proposition that they are to be faithful members and attenders of a local congregation.

They believe they can grow just fine as Christians without all the mess of a church.

Yes, the church is a messy place. It is an imperfect place. It is a place that can truly be contentious. The objections to connecting with a local congregation are many.

For certain, there are some detours. Let's look at them with clarity and honesty.

Three Questions

1. What does it mean to be a member of the body of Christ?
2. How does 1 Corinthians 13 relate to church membership?
3. Why is a *family* a good metaphor for the church?

3

Detours

"We are the Spartans!"

It has been almost half a century since I screamed those words with my high school football teammates. It was my senior year, and we were coming off a season when we had finished with an abysmal record of 2–8. Most observers believed the upcoming season would be even worse. One newspaper predicted we wouldn't win a game all year. I couldn't blame them. Our team was lousy to begin with, and we had lost some of our best players from the year before, including our quarterback.

During my junior year, I had been moved from linebacker to running back. It wasn't because I was good; we just didn't have that many options. But something happened to our team during the offseason. During the spring of my junior year, all the rising seniors gathered together to make a commitment. We would give our all to the team. We held voluntary practices in the spring and summer. We hit the weights. We ran sprints. We studied the playbook.

As a result of our commitment to one another, no one missed a practice during the grueling two-a-days at the end of the summer. We were in better shape than we had ever been. We knew the plays. We had the pass routes down. We knew our blocking assignments. And I was learning the techniques of being a running back after playing the position for only half of the previous season.

Coach John watched us work, perhaps with a bit of amusement at first. He was our third coach in five years, and he was not very popular with the local residents. They wanted a winning team, and he had not delivered. He was likely thinking this season would be his last. There was no way a team with even less talent than the terrible team of the previous year could win. But when Coach John saw our commitment, he began to catch the vision. He started encouraging us. Motivating us. Pushing us. And it was Coach John who led the cry, "We are the Spartans!"

Still, only a sparse crowd came to our first home game. They were shocked when we won and won big. The crowds grew as our team moved to 5–0. By then, we were ranked third in the state. We were surprising everyone. It was an amazing thing to see.

We are the Spartans!

I wish I could tell you we had a movie-like ending, finished undefeated, and won the state championship. That didn't happen. Instead, we lost to two perennial powerhouses later in the year and finished the regular season at 8–2. But we made it to the quarterfinals of the state championship before getting knocked out.

It was such an unlikely season, such an unexpected story. Along with our team's success, I finished fourth in the state in rushing. Our smallest lineman, all 160 pounds of him, made the all-state team. Our quarterback had never played quarterback, but he performed magnificently. Our fullback also played linebacker and was the most valuable player on the team.

We are the Spartans!

We were committed. It was tough, but we all sacrificed. We showed up even when we didn't feel like it. We put the team ahead of our individual desires.

Just like at church, right?

Not exactly.

For many, church isn't much more than an afterthought. You don't hear people shouting, "We are church members!" So, what's going on? How did the local church, the body of Christ, become an optional gathering of minimal importance? Why do so many church members consider church attendance just another activity—one that might easily be preempted by a sporting event, the local flea market, or a desire to sleep in on Sunday? Let's look at both the *what* and the *how.*

What Is Throwing Us Off Course?

The *what* includes those activities and organizations that have supplanted the church in magnitude of commitment. There are four major activities, or detours, that can throw us off course.

Detour 1: Activities for Children

I've heard a lot of families lament the scheduling of their kids' soccer games and basketball tournaments on Sunday mornings. But don't blame the sports leagues. Those organizations wouldn't schedule activities that conflict with church worship services if the parents didn't permit it, or perhaps even encourage it.

Simply stated, if Christians decided that church attendance was the priority for their children, the sports leagues would look for alternatives other than Sundays to schedule their games. Travel teams would be home by Sunday.

No, we can't blame the teams and the organizations. It's a choice the *parents* are making.

Is it really that important, then, that church be such a big deal for our kids? In a word: *yes.* The evidence is overwhelming that children who attend church are much healthier emotionally, physically, and socially. One of many studies on the topic was conducted in 2018 by two researchers at the Harvard T. H. Chan School of Public Health.[1] They focused on children and adolescents who attended weekly religious services. The results were amazing:

- They were less likely to subsequently have depressive symptoms.
- They were less likely to smoke.
- They were less likely to use illicit drugs.
- They were less likely to have a sexually transmitted disease.

One of the researchers, Ying Chen, concluded the following: "These findings are important for both our understanding of health and our understanding of parenting practices. . . . Many children are raised religiously, and our study shows that this can powerfully affect their health behaviors, mental health, and overall happiness and well-being."[2]

Wow. That same study noted that previous research had also linked church attendance to a much lower risk of premature death. The evidence is indeed overwhelming.

Another activity that consumes a lot of our children's time and attention is social media. If you have any doubt that moving our kids from being overly absorbed in their smartphones to caring about church attendance is important, read my book *The Anxious Generation Goes to Church*. I took the research from *The Anxious Generation*, the *New York Times* bestseller by Jonathan Haidt, and did additional research on churchgoing young people. Yes, our primary motivation in getting children into the church is to introduce them to an ongoing relationship with Jesus Christ. But there are many more benefits for them, both emotionally and physically.

I have no doubt that many parents get their kids involved in extracurricular activities for noble reasons. They love their children. They want them well-rounded. They want them healthy and happy. Frankly, though, some parents push their children into activities as a proxy for their own desires and dreams. The parents pursue their own athletic ambitions through their children, even if the children have no real desire to participate.

But when those activities become a detour around church involvement, parents are actually hurting their children. The absence of regular church involvement means the children are more likely to become depressed, more likely to smoke and take illicit drugs, and more likely to be at risk sexually. In our hearts, we know this is true, because the Bible tells us so: "Direct your children onto the right path, and when they are older, they will not leave it" (Proverbs 22:6).

The right path for children includes faithful church attendance. And the research backs it up.

Detour 2: Vacation and Leisure

No, I am not a vacation grinch. I love taking vacations with my family. In fact, almost every year we get all four Rainer families together for vacation. It's a crazy time with eighteen people in one place, but it's a total joy.

I like vacations. I like leisure trips. I really do. But an unsettling trend among active church members has emerged in recent years. I got a clear picture of this new reality from a friend named Charlie, who pastors a church on the Florida Panhandle. Charlie's church is about two miles from white sands and emerald waters. As you might expect, the area has become a tourist haven, and many people have built second homes and condos in the area.

"For many years," Charlie told me, "I would see a huge influx of tourists in our church in the spring and the summer seasons. It was really cool to meet people from all over the place. But we began to see the numbers drop off about five years ago."

"Why do you suppose that is?" I asked. "Are fewer tourists coming to the Panhandle these days?"

"No, not at all," Charlie responded. "Our area continues to grow with tourist traffic. In fact, it's crazier than ever. But the more I've asked around, the clearer the picture has become. Active church members aren't nearly as likely to attend worship services when they're on vacation. It's almost as if they think they should take a vacation from church as well."

I've told the story elsewhere about the profound impression made on me as a child by a family called the Archibalds. When my family went on vacation, we never attended church. We weren't that active in our home church either. But I vividly remember waking up one Sunday morning when we were vacationing with the Archibalds and finding them dressed and ready to leave for church. I remember saying that I didn't know people went to church when they were on vacation. They responded with kindness that they didn't know you *weren't* supposed to attend church while on vacation.

Vacations and leisure trips have become a detour from church involvement. And with many families having more disposable income today than they used to, they can afford to take more trips.

Detour 3: Work

A 2017 article in *Forbes* reports that 70 percent of employed Americans today work at least one weekend a month. The central theme of the article, titled "Working on the Weekend Is the New Normal and That's a Bad Thing," is that we have lost much of our leisure time. Three-fourths of respondents ages 25–44 indicated that "they couldn't stop thinking about their work on the weekends,"[3] even when they were not physically in the workplace or checking emails.

An additional major contributor to the never-off-work mentality is the rise of the entrepreneurial and self-employed society. According to another article in *Forbes*, at some point during a given week in 2019, 44 million Americans were self-employed.[4] For some, self-employment offers meaningful benefits such as flexibility, autonomy, and the satisfaction that comes from building one's own company. But the responsibility of owning a business also has its downside.

Self-employed workers often don't feel they have the luxury of taking time off like people who get a paycheck from a company. Taking time off can mean forgoing income, missing an opportunity, or failing to network. Sunday morning is still the most common time for churches to gather for worship. But for the self-employed, Sunday morning might seem like the best time to catch up on work or simply sleep in after working a long week.

Of course, overwork isn't limited to the self-employed. Those who earn a paycheck from an employer often feel compelled to work long hours as well, for a variety of reasons. They too may view Sunday mornings as an opportune time to catch up around the house, do one more thing for the company, or simply rest.

I was recently in a conversation with a pastor in Pennsylvania who was frustrated that four of his five elders had become sporadic in their worship attendance. They all had the same explanation: They were too busy at work. When the pastor gently asked if they considered the church a priority, one of the elders responded: "Of course, but you know our work has to come first."

Ouch.

More on this attitude later.

Detour 4: Time for Self and Family

Yes, we need time for ourselves. Yes, we need time to relax. Yes, we need time for our families. I get that. I agree with that. But where should that time come from?

In recent years, I've noticed a gradual but discernable shift in attitudes among active church members. Time for self, time for relaxation, and family time are often seen as competing with time for church. It hasn't always been that way.

Historically, church members saw time for self as a good way to grow as a disciple with the gathered church. Historically, church members saw their weekly commitment to gather with other believers as a biblical way to rest and focus on the things that really mattered. Historically, church members viewed taking the entire family to church as the best way to spend time with them.

For many church members today, time for self and family are viewed in opposition to time at church—a mindset contrary to the biblical view that community, significance, and purpose are to be found in the local church.

How Did We Get Here?

So *how* did all this happen? I see at least six causes.

Cause 1: Rearranged Priorities

Upon hearing that I will soon be writing my forty-second book, a friend asked, "How have you had time to write that many books?" My response may have seemed simplistic, if not a bit snarky: "I *make* time to write them."

I wasn't meaning to be flippant. But the simple reality is that I write books because I allocate time to write them. Today, I can finish a manuscript faster than I used to. Practice does that. But I still have to set aside time on my calendar for writing. If it's not on the calendar, it's not a priority. If it's not a priority, it doesn't get done.

For many church members who once were very active in their congregations, attending church has become an optional activity rather than a priority. They give the church any hours that are left over after the really important activities are accomplished. Indeed, I refer to this level of church commitment as "the leftover mentality." Simply stated, we give time to those things we deem important. For many church members, their local congregation is no longer that important.

Cause 2: More Choices

I'm old enough to remember when there was no Disney World. The famous theme park opened in 1971, when I was sixteen. For most of my childhood, I had very few choices for entertainment. A trip to the Florida Panhandle a couple of weeks a year was the most we could do or afford. I did make it to Disney World in 1972—and yes, it was magical. I was blown away.

The number of amusements and trips that are available today would have been unfathomable to me as a child. A friend of mine recently wrote a to-do list for activities in the greater Nashville area where we live. His list had more than seventy attractions and activities. In other words, a resident of Nashville could miss more than a year of church going to these places—without even leaving the local area.

As a side note, many churches tried to compete with the world of entertainment and activities to attract people to church. It worked for a season, but then the approach began to fall apart. Entertaining people is not the church's purpose. That's not where churches should focus their resources.

Cause 3: More Income

Though it may seem counterintuitive, there are a number of ways to measure household income. Is it pretax or after-tax? Does it adjust for inflation? Does it take into account the number of people in the household? Does it use median or average numbers? How do the demographics of your community affect the measurement?

Without worrying about the specifics, we can safely draw a few conclusions. First, families have more disposable income today than they had a few decades ago. Second, the growth in household income has not been evenly distributed across all households. Third, the rate of growth is clearly slowing for lower- and middle-income families.

Still, generally speaking, families have more money to spend today than they did, say, twenty years ago. Also, some previously unaffordable items, such as high-end televisions, have dropped dramatically in price. Likewise, many sources of entertainment have become more affordable. We can stay home and watch current movies and television shows to our heart's content.

To emphasize our earlier point, the intersection of greater income and increased entertainment opportunities has been a key factor in the decline in church attendance. Maybe it has contributed to your own declining commitment to your church. It's just so much easier today, and more affordable, to do other things and go other places.

Many church members are searching for meaning and purpose in entertainment, travel, and gadgets. They are not finding either one. But they seem to think if they keep trying, they will find that elusive meaning and purpose. Thus they go on more trips and vacations. They buy more unnecessary gadgets. And once again they come up empty.

Will these church members ever realize that their true fulfillment and purpose can come only by serving Christ through the local church? Will they ever realize that satisfaction is not found in a vacation or an item of entertainment, but it is found in the community of believers in the local church?

Will they ever return to church? As of yet, most have not.

Cause 4: Cultural Shifts

If you're older than thirty, my guess is that you've noticed a dramatic shift in recent years in our culture's attitude toward church involvement. Twenty years ago, in most regions of the United States, the general perspective of church attendance was largely positive. Being part of a local congregation was seen as a good thing.

In fact, if you weren't active in a church, you didn't necessarily want to draw attention to that fact. You would have kept your lack of involvement quiet lest you reap the disapproval of your neighbors.

Today, the tables have turned, clearly and decisively. Society at large couldn't care less if you're involved or uninvolved at church. In fact, your neighbors, friends, and coworkers would scarcely notice, much less comment, if you dropped out of church altogether.

In some sectors of the culture, the attitude toward churchgoing has not merely turned from positive to neutral or indifferent; it has turned from positive to negative. There are pockets of our society that are both anti-church and anti-Christian.

The point for our discussion here is that it is no longer a cultural taboo not to attend church. It is easy to become less active or even leave the church. And this societal attitude contributes to the challenge in local congregations of diminishing commitment by church members.

Nevertheless, the local church, with all of its problems and conflicts, is still God's plan A to reach and minister to the world. Likewise, it is God's plan A for our finding meaning, community, purpose, and significance.

When people I meet learn what I do and what I write about, they are usually quite open to discussing matters of faith and church. Jack was no exception. When I met him about a year ago, he was a Christian with nominal church involvement. He eagerly accepted my invitations to our community group and to worship services. During the pandemic, he was consistently in our weekly Zoom Bible study as well as the streaming worship services.

I have been fascinated to watch Jack grow as a believer. He is convinced that getting involved in our church has been instrumental in this growth. I can see the change in his life. I can see that Christ is using his connection to our church to bring him a newfound joy and purpose. He now has a community that surrounds him spiritually and prays for him.

Here's the point: Jack was under no cultural pressure to get involved with a church. He could have continued with his nominal Christianity. But he discovered that connecting with and serving alongside a community of believers is both good for him and good for others.

The culture is not going to help the church with its waning commitment levels. The culture is not going to support or encourage church involvement. But churches throughout history have often been the most effective when they are countercultural.

And people who become truly connected and involved with the church will discover a new sense of purpose and joy.

Just ask Jack.

Cause 5: Church Capitulation

I wish I could point to a single moment or a major event that shifted churches from expecting commitment from their members to capitulating to the culture. I know that's a strong statement. And I know there are exceptions. But many churches seem to have given up. Many churches seem willing to take the leftovers from members instead of expecting church to be a top priority.

Perhaps you have been moving toward reduced commitment in your church. As you think about where you are now, you realize that there has been very little said or done to encourage you to a higher level of commitment. It's almost as if the church is okay with your modest involvement.

Sports teams expect commitment. Civic organizations expect commitment. Nonprofit boards expect commitment. Why not churches? Why have churches become conspicuously silent about member expectations?

Though I have my ideas about the reasons for this strange attitude among churches, the real issue is that most congregations have low expectations. It is incredibly sad that the one organization God left to carry out his mission on earth has, in many ways, capitulated to the culture it is supposed to reach and change.

Many churches have dumbed down the meaning of church membership to such a degree that it has become meaningless. Some church leaders and members even declare that church membership itself is not a valid concept. The apostle Paul would disagree. Check out 1 Corinthians 12 again to see the biblical meaning of church membership.

The reasons for declining commitment among church members have three major streams. First, many church members have decided that commitment to their church is not important. Second, the culture in which we live makes it easy and acceptable not to be committed to a church. Third, many churches have lowered their expectations of members. Who wants to be part of a group that doesn't care whether or not you make a difference?

Cause 6: The COVID-19 Pandemic

The pandemic didn't help with the problem of church commitment. In fact, some would argue that the pandemic was a major contributor to the waning commitment we see today.

It's true that for months, church members couldn't gather in person to worship together. Many people watched streaming services online, but those lacked the dynamic fellowship of in-person gatherings. New habits were formed. You could watch a worship service in your pajamas. You didn't have to battle with the kids to get them ready for church. Sunday could really be a day off without the hassle of going to the church building. In other words, minimal commitment became easy for church members.

Though I understand that viewpoint, I have a different perspective. I believe the trend lines were in place before the pandemic ever happened. The problems related to COVID-19 were *catalysts* more than they were causes. In other words, we eventually would have arrived where we are today, but the pandemic and quarantine shifted the trend toward declining commitment into fast-forward. COVID-19 didn't *cause* the decline in commitment; it merely accelerated it.

Are We Really Looking for Something More?

My personal testimony is one of chasing the wrong solutions, especially in my youth and young adult years. I was seeking *something*, but all the solutions offered by our culture were to no avail.

Then shortly after Nellie Jo and I married, and just before the birth of our first child, I got involved in a church. It was the first time I had really connected with a church since becoming a Christian as a teenager. I got involved in a Bible study group. I attended worship services without exception. I was in a prayer ministry. And I was involved in outreach ministries to our community.

I did not feel *compelled* to be involved; I *wanted* to be involved. My connection to and involvement in my church was spiritual nourishment. It did not drain me; it energized me. At least intuitively, I knew I was part of something much bigger than I could ever do on my own. I was on a mission for God. I was truly finding community and purpose. I was finding something more.

On those occasions when I felt discouraged or frustrated with my church, it was typically because I was asking what the church was doing for *me*. But when I sought to be a giver rather than a receiver, I truly discovered something more.

Still, I realized pretty quickly that my church wasn't perfect. Indeed, the churches where I later served as pastor weren't perfect. As my youngest son, Jess, once pointed out, there was no way those churches could have been perfect, because I was the pastor.

There's no way to avoid the fact that churches have some real problems. The more you get involved in a church, the more clearly you will see the negative issues. But that is true of any organization, workplace, or family.

Let's agree, then, that no church will ever be perfect. Let's agree that every church will have a number of problems. We will look at those pain points shortly. For now, let's ask the question of whether the church is really the place where we can find significance, community, and purpose. The Bible is overwhelmingly clear that it is.

Three Questions

1. Why do you think becoming involved in a church is so important for a child's emotional, spiritual, and physical health?
2. Review the detours that veer us away from greater church commitment. Which ones have been struggles for you?
3. How do you think the aftermath of the COVID-19 pandemic will affect the church over the next decade?

4

"But the Church Has Problems!"

Some churches have more problems than others, but every church has its problems. My own story illustrates this painful reality.

I became a follower of Christ as a teenager after my high school football coach shared the gospel with me. My entry into a local church, however, was problematic. Well, that's an understatement. My entry into a local church as a Christian was catastrophic.

I had already been attending church somewhat regularly with my family before I became a Christian. As a new believer, however, I had a strong desire to connect with other Christians in a fresh way. But our church was a mess. I have vivid and painful memories of a three-hour church business meeting where the church ultimately voted to split. I remember people calling each other names. Crying. Walking out. Even bursts of profanity. It was terrible.

Still, I hung in there and followed my family to the breakaway church. And guess what happened? That church split too.

Are you kidding me?

I was done with church attendance at that point. As a young teenager, I wanted my freedom and space from a lot of things, especially church. My parents did not try to convince me otherwise. It was hard to argue that the church was where I ought to be after all we had experienced.

You can predict what happened in my life from that point forward. I was truly a baby Christian in need of guidance and accountability. Without the influence of other believers in a local church, I became rebellious. I turned to partying and defying any and all forms of authority.

At one point, I was expelled from high school for some of my actions. I appeared before the school board and begged for another chance. They showed a bit of mercy and changed the expulsion to suspension with a number of remedial actions for me to take.

I was absolutely miserable, but I went to college with that same rebellious mindset. My lifestyle was still terrible. When my girlfriend (my future wife) arrived at the same college a year later, she decided she couldn't deal with the party life at the school or with me. So she left. I was devastated.

Nellie Jo's departure was not an immediate wake-up call, but it was the beginning of a turnaround for me. I was hurt. My pain was palpable. If I had been wise and walking with God, I would have seen myself as a prodigal son in need of returning immediately to the open arms of the Father.

Instead of growing spiritually, I made the decision to focus on my studies and grow academically. Which was not all bad—though I would have done much better to have prayed, read my Bible, and connected with a church. Still, dedicating myself to school began a process of removing me from some of the influences that were contributing to my rebellion. It was a decent first step, but far from perfect.

Yes, I was a Christian, but still a baby Christian. I had not matured in my faith at all. But Nellie Jo's transfer to another college was a catalyst for change. Though I did not find a local church immediately, Christ began the work of altering my lifestyle. As I poured myself into my studies instead of partying, my life began to change—sometimes slowly, sometimes backtracking, but persistently changing.

Though I didn't know at the time what Nellie Jo was thinking, she later shared with me her doubts about our relationship. For a few years, she had assumed we would get married. But seeing the way I was living, she began to wonder if I was really in God's plan for her life. I guess when she saw the change in my lifestyle it gave her some hope. And though I still needed to make more changes, she accepted my marriage proposal.

After we got married, Nellie Jo began gently nudging me to find a church home for us. When we found out she was pregnant with our first child, that was the clincher for me. I was a husband and about to become a dad. I knew I had to become the spiritual leader of our home.

That doesn't mean the transition to church life was smooth and easy. Not at all. You see, I soon discovered that churches were still not perfect.

"The Church Is Full of Hypocrites!"

We found a church home we absolutely loved a few months before Sam was born, and I finally began to grow as a Christian. The preaching was great. The pastors are still my friends forty years later. There were no arguments about worship style. Or if those arguments took place, I didn't know about them.

As a young adult, I was discovering that the Christian life was never meant to be a solo adventure. God gave us a local church where we could worship, make friends, enjoy fellowship, grow as disciples, be held accountable, and become witnesses to others. Nellie Jo and I were at the church facilities regularly.

I received eternal life when I became a follower of Christ, but I knew he wanted me to have an abundant life as well. I was starting to catch on. A life of significance was inextricably tied to the local church.

For reasons I don't recall, Nellie Jo and I made the decision to join separate small groups (we called them Sunday school classes back then) instead of going together to a couples class. She joined a group of young women, and I was in a class with all guys. I suspect Nellie Jo knew I would be more open and comfortable there.

My friendship with those young men was a powerful influence in my life. I knew I was growing as a believer. I started showing up at the church at 5:00 a.m. on Tuesdays for an hour of prayer. I was happy to get up early and then return home to see my wife and son wake up. Connecting to a local church turned out to be the missing piece in my life.

Then disaster struck. Okay, that's a bit of hyperbole, but it felt like a disaster at the time.

I was at the grocery store one day and saw my small group leader. He had his back to me and was talking to someone else. I don't recall his exact words, but I remember quite vividly that they were interspersed with profanity.

I was devastated. I turned and left before he ever saw me. I went home and told Nellie Jo about the hypocrite in the church—and a Sunday school teacher at that. I wasn't sure I could return to the class, and maybe not even the church. I had trouble grasping what I had seen and heard. It wasn't how "good church people" were supposed to act.

Nellie Jo responded by telling me about her lifelong experience in a local church. She shared with me the hypocrisy of some of the church members she had observed while growing up. Some of them, too, were in leadership positions. She also told me that sometimes *she* was the hypocrite. She made mistakes. She sinned.

Then she told me in a calm but firm voice that I was a hypocrite as well. I didn't always live a life that was exemplary and God-honoring. She wasn't being condescending, and she wasn't lecturing me. She was being factual. She was being truthful for my own good.

Ouch.

Her rebuttal was painful, but necessary. It was another major turning point in my life as a believer in Christ. Instead of lamenting the hypocrites, I started praying for them. Instead of judging others, I tried to become an example to them. Instead of bemoaning every flaw I saw in others, I asked God to work on fixing *my* flaws.

And all the while, I remained a hypocrite in the church. In other words, I did not attain sinless perfection. I believe I grew as a Christian, but I was a long way from full maturity. Still, I learned how to live among and love my fellow hypocrites in the church. Works in progress, all of us.

The New Testament doesn't sugarcoat the issue of hypocrisy in the church. Indeed, most of 1 and 2 Corinthians deals with sinful and hypocritical church members. My favorite New Testament book is Philippians. It has so many references to joy and unity. I get a smile on my face every time I read it.

But even in that unified and joyous church, there was

hypocrisy in the congregation. We don't know the details of the conflict between two church members named Euodia and Syntyche. But it was enough of a problem that Paul wrote about them in his letter to the church: "I appeal to Euodia and Syntyche. Please, because you belong to the Lord, settle your disagreement" (Philippians 4:2).

Sometimes I feel sorry for Euodia and Syntyche. How would you like to be immortalized in Scripture because you were in a church fight with another member? You don't hear of many kids being named for those two.

There will always be hypocrites in the church, because we are all sinners. There will always be issues in the church. You will have hypocrites in your own family, including you. But that is no reason to abandon those you love.

To the contrary, the Bible is clear that we are to love one another. We are to pray for one another. We are to serve one another. We are to put others first. And the "others" in these mandates are not perfect. They are sinners and hypocrites. Just like you and me.

"I Am Not Getting Fed"

I can't help but feel sorry for pastors on this issue. For years in the past, church members compared their pastors' preaching to radio and television pastors. Today, pastors are compared to podcast pastors and YouTube pastors and pastors whose sermons are shared on social media.

Here is an email forwarded to me by a member of the Church Answers community. He received this email on a Monday after he preached his Sunday sermon:

> Pastor, I was really excited when you announced you would be preaching through the book of Romans. It's my favorite book of the Bible. When you preached the first sermon yesterday on Romans 1:1-17, I was disappointed. You missed some key doctrinal points and really did not do the text justice. I suggest you listen to [name of podcast pastor] on his sermon series through Romans. It would help you to get it right. We really do need to be fed better.
>
> Your friend,

Sigh. What a wonderful friend.

Okay, I get it. Pastors need to be diligent about feeding their congregations. They certainly need to put time and prayer into sermon and teaching preparation. But no pastor can meet all the expectations of every member. Most pastors can't compare to someone's favorite podcast preacher.

If you've read my other books, you know that Frances Mason was my favorite church member when I served as a pastor. Though I never considered myself the best preacher in the world, I did put time and prayer into my sermons.

Yet, after one particular sermon I felt terrible. I knew I had bombed. I shared my frustration with Frances.

"I got a lot out of your sermon," she responded. "I have learned that if I ask God to teach me something every time someone preaches or teaches the Bible, God always answers my prayers. It's not just the preacher's responsibility to prepare; we who are being taught must also prepare ourselves. A listening heart is just as important as a teaching heart."

To be honest, there have been times when I have walked away with a critical spirit after hearing a sermon. I've even had the audacity to mentally rehearse how I would have done it better. Most of the time, however, the Holy Spirit checks my heart and attitude. And then I remember Frances. Her attitude and words of encouragement both convict me and inspire me. Then I repent and pray for my pastor.

May those with a Frances Mason attitude increase in number in our churches!

"The Pastor Doesn't Meet My Needs"

The community I lead at Church Answers includes some of the brightest and most godly church leaders I have ever known. They are, however, completely and utterly human. They struggle with church member expectations.

A pastor I'll call Greg shared with the community a particular example of pastoral expectations. His subject line was something like "A day in the life of a pastor."

His ministry day began at 8:00 a.m. with a call from an irate church member. She had been in the hospital for two days (well, one night, he later discovered). Her issue wasn't serious, but she had expected the pastor to visit her.

When Greg immediately told her he was on his way to the hospital to see her, she told him she had been released two days earlier.

"I didn't even know you were in the hospital," he said.

"You should have known."

So pastors need omniscience.

Greg also had a personal issue he was watching closely. His wife was due any day with their second child. As it happened, "any day" began two hours later, when his wife informed him it was time to go to the hospital. At 9:30 that evening, she gave birth to their second daughter.

Obviously caught up in the moment, Greg didn't check his phone, where he had set a reminder that he had promised to be at a Sunday school class fellowship at 6:00 p.m. When he finally looked at his phone around midnight, there was a text from the person who had invited him to the fellowship: "I know you were at the hospital, but you could have at least dropped by."

So pastors need to be omnipresent. In fact, most pastors and church staff members would do so much better if they were omniscient, omnipresent, and also omnipotent. Then they would not only be able to read people's minds to know what every church member wants, but they would also have the ability to be everywhere at once with the power to meet every need.

That would pretty much solve every problem between the pastor and the congregation. My approach here is obviously tongue in cheek, but the problem is no laughing matter for most pastors.

To begin with, it's important to understand that these complaints arise from an unbiblical view of church leadership. Many church members see the pastor as their personal spiritual and emotional guide. They may also see him as the "church manager," the one responsible for every activity, meeting, and need that occurs within the life of the congregation.

But let's return to Acts 6, when the church was still very young and fragile, to see how the leaders handled a complaint that a group of widows was not receiving adequate ministry from the church.

> As the believers rapidly multiplied, there were rumblings of discontent. The Greek-speaking believers complained about the Hebrew-speaking believers, saying that their widows were being discriminated against in the daily distribution of food.
>
> **ACTS 6:1**

A typical response by many pastors would be to try to meet the need themselves. After all, how many times has a pastor heard, "That's what we pay you to do"?

The leaders of the early church, however, knew that the congregation would lose its spiritual momentum if leadership assumed responsibility for every ministry. It was physically impossible for them to have their hands on everything. Their solution, therefore, was basic. They equipped and ordained others to do the work of ministry, beginning with seven trusted deacons.

The leaders were also straightforward about their priorities: "We apostles should spend our time teaching the word of God, not running a food program" (Acts 6:2). Well, there you go.

The model was established. The biblical priority was clear. The leaders' responsibility "is to equip God's people to do his work and build up the church, the body of Christ" (Ephesians 4:12).

We have forgotten that biblical pattern in many of our churches. Instead, it looks more like this:

- The pastor is to minister to me personally.
- The pastor is to visit me regularly.
- The pastor is to attend every meeting.
- The pastor is to attend all church social functions.

You get the picture. Many church members see their churches as imperfect and problem-filled because they have unreasonable expectations of the pastor. So they either move to another church with their same unmet expectations, or they drop out of church altogether. After all, the pastor didn't meet their needs.

"All They Talk About Is Money"

I began hearing this complaint with frequency in the 1970s, with the rise in prominence of televangelists. It has not abated since.

It seems the more recent cacophony is related to some celebrity pastors who have had issues of financial impropriety, among other problems. Some have also taught a prosperity gospel, giving rise to many more complaints.

Unfortunately, the abuses by a few preachers become fodder for more criticism, often directed at local churches and their pastors. Though my observations are anecdotal, I have rarely heard a pastor or other church leader overemphasize money. Sure, there are exceptions, but they are rare.

At the same time, money, stewardship, and generosity should not be topics on which pastors are silent. Many, however, avoid the topic of finances lest they hear the oft-repeated criticism, "All they talk about is money."

Frankly, most pastors need to talk about money a lot

more often than they do. Jesus talked about money in eleven of his parables. He taught that we should give our money to support the religious institutions that God established. (See, for example, Matthew 23:23 and Mark 12:41-44.) By the time the first church was established in Jerusalem, it became obvious that the local church would be the conduit through which believers gave of their resources.

The priorities of the local church are clearly and powerfully stated in Acts 2:42: "All the believers devoted themselves to the apostles' teaching, and to fellowship, and to sharing in meals (including the Lord's Supper), and to prayer."

But shortly after these high priorities were established, the church members also began giving: "All the believers met together in one place and shared everything they had. They sold their property and possessions and shared the money with those in need" (Acts 2:44-45).

Far from "all they ever talk about is money," the reality is that we don't hear enough about giving and stewardship in the local church. The sins of a few leaders have resulted in the silence of far too many others.

Quite frankly, the excuse that there's an overemphasis on money is just that: an excuse. At best, it is based on false perceptions. More often than not, this complaint comes from people who are not actively involved in a church. Those who are know the truth.

"The Church Is Wherever God's People Are"

The church is a family. We discussed this metaphor earlier. Now imagine if you used the excuse that "the family is wherever our people are" to never get together with your children, siblings, and parents. Think what would happen if you told your spouse and children that you don't have to spend time with them because you're still a family no matter where you are. In all likelihood, your family would not do well.

What is the meaning of *family* if its members don't get together?

Likewise, the church is meant to gather. The church is prescribed to gather. The church is not the church unless it gathers. Let's return to the model and example of the Jerusalem church. Luke, the author of Acts, does not waste words. He is very careful in everything he writes in the Gospel of Luke and in Acts.

So when he describes the first congregation, he uses the same precision to remind us that the people of the church were together, in person: "All the believers met together in one place and shared everything they had" (Acts 2:44). Again, he describes their corporate worship as a gathered worship: "They worshiped together at the Temple each day, met in homes for the Lord's Supper, and shared their meals with great joy and generosity" (Acts 2:46).

They were together. Church members are members of the church wherever they are. But the church is not the church unless it gathers together.

The word often used for church in the Greek New Testament is *ekklesia*. It appears more than one hundred times in the New Testament. It was originally used in common Greek culture to denote meetings convened at a public place for the purpose of deliberating. The early church adopted the word in the same sense: an assembly of Christians gathered for worship.

Of course, the use of *ekklesia* takes on different nuances in the New Testament, but at its heart is the sense of gathering.

Today, some have asked whether the digital church can replace our need for an in-person church. The pandemic certainly demonstrated how digital technology can be an instrument for God's work. Churches that were not able to meet in person had streaming worship services on Facebook, YouTube, and other platforms.

Similarly, many church-based groups continued to meet on the various videoconferencing platforms. Like the Roman roads that were a literal pathway for spreading the gospel in the first century, the internet has become a conduit for evangelism in the twenty-first century. Digital tools will certainly be used with greater intensity and frequency in the years ahead. The possibilities are seemingly endless.

But while the digital church has certainly expanded the reach and influence of many congregations, it can't fully replace the in-person experience. We would not want to replace our family time with only digital experiences. The church is designed to be a family that meets together in person.

For some, though, this so-called problem is not directly tied to the digital church. Some object when anyone suggests the need to "go to church." They will immediately say that the church is wherever God's people are; the church, they say, is not a place to go.

In some sense, that objection is a bit of theological nitpicking. I get it. "Going to church" is not the most precise way to define a weekly gathering. But I think it would be more confusing if we used phrases like "go to the gathered church." When people say they are "going to church," most often they mean attending a worship service.

The essence of the objection, though, is that regular church gatherings are unnecessary for the church today. That objection, plainly speaking, is simply not true. Nowhere—absolutely nowhere—in the New Testament is there any indication that it is optional for the church to gather.

Yes, the church is the church beyond its weekly gatherings. The church is certainly the church in the community, in the marketplace, and in our places of employment. Yes, the church is the church wherever God's people are. But the church is not the church unless it gathers, as well. That is simply what the Bible tells us.

"The Church Is Toxic"

Occasionally, the objection to attending the gathered church is a broad but intense concern. The church is *toxic*, some say. Critics attest to congregations so divided, so angry, and so self-centered that it is all but impossible to worship and function as a healthy and growing disciple there.

But is there any truth to this claim? Are some churches so immersed in their negativity that they are unable and unwilling to carry out their mission?

Some critics will declare that a church is toxic when it doesn't do exactly what they think it should. Still, there are some situations where the health of a church has deteriorated greatly. Those churches hardly look like churches anymore.

Toxicity in a church can flow from church members, church leaders, or both. Some members can treat the church like it's their personal service organization. They seem determined to keep outsiders from entering or joining. They push only for their own preferences.

Many times they are determined to gain and keep control. If the church has business meetings, they seek to drive the agenda, while other members remain silent from fear or resignation. These churches are totally inwardly focused. The occasional guest might get the sense that the church should have posted a No Trespassing sign out front. Often, bullies control the church and seek to control the other members.

Likewise, church leaders can be toxic. Their traits can be similar to those of toxic church members, but they have the power advantage of leadership and the bully pulpit. Indeed,

I have seen a number of situations where a toxic pastor and toxic members have collided. It was not a pretty sight.

My point is simply that churches can become so toxic that they create an organization that, for all biblical purposes, is not a church. Thankfully, these churches are the exception, not the rule. So when this issue is raised as a reason not to be active in a local congregation, my suggestion is that the concerned individual find one of the countless other churches that functions biblically. Out of an estimated 350,000 congregations in the United States, there are certainly a lot of unhealthy churches; but truly toxic churches are few in number.

Simply stated, if you happen to encounter a toxic church, don't give up on all churches everywhere. Find a healthier church.

From Problems to Possibilities

It's time to move on from the problems to start looking at the possibilities. We have been given abundant life by Jesus Christ, and he wants us to live it fully. That abundant life can be fully realized when we join together with other Christians in community, ministry, and purpose. The nexus where we find that connection is called the church.

As you have no doubt gleaned by now, I like to look at the first church in Jerusalem for some key ideas about church life. The congregation was fresh from their encounter at Pentecost. They had discovered and realized the work of the Holy Spirit in their lives. Now they were ready to reach the world together. Now they were ready to have a life of significance together.

Luke is indeed precise in his writing about this early church in his narrative in Acts. He does not waste a word. As the Jerusalem church was gathering, growing, giving, and joining on mission together, Luke gives us a glimpse of how the outside world was viewing them. He simply says they were "enjoying the goodwill of all the people" (Acts 2:47).

Becoming involved in a local church is how God designed for us to find significance and meaning. For sure, we reap the benefits of living lives that are different and dynamic. But Luke wants us to see this truth clearly: It isn't just that our lives are different; it's that our lives make a difference.

We can bemoan the problems of local congregations. We can create a litany of excuses for why we should not be connected to a church. We can point to problems, hypocrites, and sloppy ministry.

Or we can take a different approach. We can see that God designed the local church for believers to be on mission together. We can see that most of the spiritual growth in the New Testament takes place in the context of a local church. We can see that, despite the flaws and mistakes of every believer from the first century till now, God is still using local congregations as the instrument by which his Spirit grows people into more mature followers of Christ.

And don't miss this reality: The early church described in the New Testament changed the world. Indeed, it turned the world upside down. Yes, there were problems with people such as Euodia and Syntyche and dozens more, both named and unnamed in the Bible. We can focus on the hard cases and hypocrites if we want.

But if we read the New Testament to see the real influence and impact of the church, we will inevitably conclude that the church (and its members) really did change the world. God's purpose hasn't changed. He has given our local churches the mandate to do nothing less—we must change our world too.

And you can be absolutely certain about this promise: If you get on board with God's purpose and plan, you will be a part of his work to change the world. Yes, *you* will change the world.

Could there be anything more significant than changing the world? The life of significance is meant to unfold in the context of community. The life of significance is designed to be lived out in the local church. That's what we mean when we say we are on mission together.

I told my own story at the beginning of this chapter. It's the story of a new believer trying to figure out his purpose in this world apart from the community of the local church.

But that story was a nonstarter. My real story did not begin until I discovered what God wanted for my life by becoming connected to a local church.

Only then did I discover the different paths God had for me. Only when I completely embraced that imperfect community called the local church did I begin to discover a life of significance.

Let's dive more deeply into this concept by examining five crucial commitments that every church member should make if we want the local church to function as God intended.

Three Questions

1. Why do you think "hypocrisy in the church" is the excuse most often used by people who don't attend church?
2. Why can't the ungathered church really be a church?
3. See Philippians 4:2-3. What do you think the situation was with Euodia and Syntyche?

Part 2

Five Crucial Commitments

They are often the quiet ones.

They are the church members who understand that their imperfect congregation can still be used by God to change the world.

Even if they have an extroverted and fun personality, you won't hear them boasting of their work for their church or their generosity for the congregation.

But they get it. When they make a difference as church members, they make a difference for God's Kingdom and glory.

I called one such member a few days ago. His name is John. He is a member of a church where I served as pastor many years ago. I remembered him as fun, boisterous, and always on the move. But he was always quiet about how he loved and supported the church. It was important to John that he receive none of the glory.

Even as pastor, I didn't know the full details of John's life and commitment. I wasn't privy to giving records in the church, but I had a lot of anecdotal evidence to suggest he was very generous. When our church started a second campus, he asked me how much the start-up costs would be. I never heard from him again on the topic, but the campus was fully funded.

When a church member named Jim died, John was already with the widow before I got there. Similar stories repeated themselves throughout my ministry.

John had many commitments, including running his own successful company. But he was never too busy for the church.

Much to my shame, I went many years without staying in touch with John. When I finally made the call, he was happy to hear from me. He told me he was eighty-five years old now and "slowing down a bit." His voice wasn't as strong, but I immediately recognized the strength in his spirit, even over the phone.

I thanked John for the crucial commitments he had made to his church. I thanked him for his kindness and his support of me. I could tell he was uncomfortable with my words. He wanted no credit. He didn't want a spotlight. He repeatedly shifted the conversation to ask questions about my family and me.

John is a longstanding and committed church member, and he changed the world through his church. His name is not recorded in Hebrews 11, but he is still a hero of the faith.

The Commitment of the Early Church Members

The earliest Christians, from the very beginning, understood that following Christ meant radical devotion. The book of

Acts paints a vivid picture of believers who were willing to sacrifice their comfort, their reputation, their possessions, and even their lives for the sake of the gospel. In the days after Pentecost, these new disciples embraced a life of wholehearted commitment: "All the believers devoted themselves to the apostles' teaching, and to fellowship, and to sharing in meals (including the Lord's Supper), and to prayer" (Acts 2:42).

This devotion wasn't casual participation; it was a fervent, whole-life dedication to living out their faith in tangible ways. Their generosity went well beyond a weekly meeting or a nominal association with the church. Luke notes: "They sold their property and possessions and shared the money with those in need" (Acts 2:45).

Many gave sacrificially, not out of abundance but out of conviction that God would use their resources to care for the poor, fund missionary efforts, and strengthen the entire faith community. They took seriously the unity described in Acts 4:32: "All the believers were united in heart and mind. And they felt that what they owned was not their own, so they shared everything they had."

Such generosity was not always comfortable. Acts 5 recounts the cautionary story of Ananias and Sapphira, who tried to deceive the church about their giving. Their tragic end underscored how the early church valued honesty, purity of heart, and openhanded stewardship of God's resources. This was not about compulsory giving or showy displays of piety, but a heartfelt response to God's grace—a willingness to say, "All I have is God's, and I want to use it for his glory."

Sacrificial commitment also meant serving the overlooked and marginalized. In Acts 6, when certain widows were neglected in the daily distribution of food, the apostles appointed seven men—often regarded as the first deacons—to ensure that every widow received care. This step showed how the earliest believers did not view service as optional; it was integral to the church's mission.

The pastoral letters echo these themes of sacrificial commitment. In 1 and 2 Timothy and Titus, Paul instructs church leaders to model hospitality, integrity, and concern for the needy. Rather than seeking personal gain, they were to be "above reproach," leading by example so that the congregation would flourish in generous living.

Moreover, Paul frequently praised congregations for their active love and financial support. He thanked the Philippians for their gifts, calling them "a sweet-smelling sacrifice that is acceptable and pleasing to God" (Philippians 4:18). In 2 Corinthians 8–9, he points to the Macedonian believers, who, despite their own poverty, overflowed in rich generosity. Their example challenged others to give willingly and cheerfully, driven by gratitude for "the generous grace of our Lord Jesus Christ" (2 Corinthians 8:9).

Through persecution, scarcity, and spiritual warfare, these early Christians found joy in their sacrificial commitments.

Their giving and serving were rooted in profound thankfulness for their salvation. As we consider these believers—many of whose names we don't even know—we see the same steadfast spirit that animates modern disciples like my friend John: quiet, unwavering, and fully devoted to God's Kingdom. This is the power of a church whose members are all-in for Christ.

Crucial Commitments and Joy

Don't miss it.

As the early Christians served and sacrificed, they did so with joy. As my friend John served and sacrificed without hesitation, he did so with joy. In fact, John is one of the most joyous people I know.

When you make five crucial commitments to your church, you will change the world—to the glory of God. And do you know what else will happen? You will discover an irrepressible, overflowing joy.

Of course, you don't make these commitments primarily for your own benefit. Your motive is not a selfish one. But there is no joy quite like serving Christ through a local congregation. Indeed, it will change your life for good as you, through the power of God, change the world for good.

The early church members got it. John gets it.

These five commitments are crucial for God's glory here on earth. And they are crucial for your joy.

To be clear, this is not a legalistic checklist, nor is it comprehensive. But the five crucial commitments we will discuss in the next several chapters are representative of what our research has shown are key characteristics of committed members in healthy churches.

I hope you will take the time to consider them carefully.

5

Radical Prayer

A radical Christian is a normal Christian.

By "normal," I mean someone who defines what it means to be a Christian, according to the Bible.

A radical Christian is one whose faith is transformative. They are different from most people in the surrounding culture. They illuminate a clear path for others; thus they are called *light*. They enhance the flavor of life while preserving what is true and good; thus they are called *salt*.

Their commitment to Jesus Christ and his commands is intense. At least it appears that way to outside observers.

The term *radical* comes from the Latin *radix*, meaning "root." A radical Christian is one who goes back to the root of their faith—Jesus, his life, and his teachings.

Radical Christian behavior manifests itself in different ways. A commitment to prayer is one of those ways. Thus, radical prayer is the first of the five crucial commitments every church member should make. Radical prayer can transform the world, the local community—and the church member who makes the commitment.

Radical prayer is rooted in the faith described in Hebrews 11:1: "Faith shows the reality of what we hope for; it is the evidence of things we cannot see."

Radical Praying Heroes

I also have my own personal heroes of the faith—specifically, church members whose lives have intersected with mine. I mentioned John in the previous chapter, and other names come quickly to mind: Lillian Anderson, Aulene Maxwell, Frances Mason, and Paul Hughey. I could easily extend the list to include many more church members who have enriched my life over the years, but these four stand out for a specific reason: They prayed for me and others in the church regularly, faithfully, and sacrificially.

I have learned much from my heroes. They taught me the priority of prayer. They taught me the power of prayer. They taught me the faithfulness of consistency in prayer. Indeed, they taught me that prayer is the major difference between churches that struggle and churches that thrive.

Do you want to live a life of significance? Commit yourself to being a church member who prays.

Not one of the five church members I mentioned was a high-profile leader in the church. In fact, I sometimes wondered if they felt unappreciated in their ministries. Their service to the church was rarely highlighted. I can't recall a single time when any of them drew a large crowd with their ministries.

Still, they persisted. If they grew weary, I didn't see it. In fact, they seemed to know when I was weary, and they would let me know they were praying for my strength.

They were—and are—my heroes.

Prayer may be the most neglected ministry in the church. Prayer may be the greatest need in the church. God has called you as a believer and as a church member to be a person of prayer.

I love how Paul addresses the members of the Thessalonian church with three brief but powerful commands: "Always be joyful. Never stop praying. Be thankful in all circumstances, for this is God's will for you who belong to Christ Jesus" (1 Thessalonians 5:16-18).

Joy, *prayer*, and *gratitude* are three powerful characteristics of a person who lives a life of significance. Each of those components is to be practiced continually: Paul says, "Always . . . never stop . . . in all circumstances."

Prayer is the centerpiece.

How, then, do we put prayer into action in our churches? What are the practical implications for those who truly desire to live a life of significance? Here are some of the applications I learned from my faith heroes, as well as from many other church members and leaders. In the context of the local church, I've found that radically praying church members pray in distinct ways.

Pray for Yourself

He came into my study broken and on the edge of tears. When he made the appointment to see me, I admit I felt a surge of dread. He was one of my chief critics. I had lost count of the issues for which he had criticized me. He would even show up in the church parking lot to record when I arrived and when I left. Seriously.

His attitude had always seemed haughty and self-righteous. But not this day. His demeanor was different, his posture changed, and his tone was certainly different.

He told me he had begun praying more consistently. Previously, his prayers had mostly been pleas for God to correct and change others. But as his prayer life became more disciplined, God had begun working on him as well.

My critic now saw himself more clearly—and he didn't like what he saw. He didn't like who he had become. He came to my office with one agenda: to ask forgiveness. He didn't stay long. He told me he had others to whom he also needed to apologize and ask for forgiveness.

Wow.

One of the most powerful ways you can make a difference in your church is by committing yourself to prayer. And the most powerful way to start is by praying for yourself—specifically that God would reveal himself and his will to you, that he would convict you of attitudes and behaviors unworthy of a child of God, and that he would direct you in the way you should go.

It's amazing what God can do when we ask for his will to be done in our lives. Instead of blaming others for the problems in the church, we begin to focus on where *we* need to change. Instead of being constant critics, we become persistent encouragers. Instead of lamenting what others aren't doing in the church, we start asking what *we* can do.

Pray for your attitude—that you would be an encourager to fellow church members and to the leaders in the church.

Pray for discernment—that you would know how to respond to others and their needs.

Pray for wisdom—that you would have the mind of Christ for the many opportunities and situations in the church.

Pray for empathy—that God would put you in others' shoes so you can understand them better and serve them more meaningfully.

Remember the attitude of my former critic who came into my study. He asked me for forgiveness because he had prayed for forgiveness for himself. It's amazing how many people and situations will come to mind as you seek God's forgiveness. This man told me he kept seeing Matthew 6:14-15 in his mind's eye: "If you forgive those who sin against you, your Father will forgive you. But if you refuse to forgive others, your Father will not forgive your sins."

A ministry of prayer is imperative for living a life of significance. Let that prayer begin where God will shape you and change you.

Pray for Your Pastor

Most church members have no idea about the challenges pastors face. They assume their pastor spends a few hours each week preparing sermons and visiting people. They don't realize most pastors never truly clock out; they're effectively on call twenty-four hours a day, and someone is always scrutinizing their every move.

Consider a couple of examples.

Aaron pastors a church in Missouri. After about four years in that role, he began a series of video calls with me. I served as his coach, offering advice and insights. In these sessions, I often found myself doing more listening than speaking. Most pastors are lonely and need someone to hear them out and understand.

I don't record my coaching conversations, but I remember Aaron's words clearly, perhaps because of the depth of his pain. The conversation started with a common question among pastors: "What can I do about Facebook critics?"

He explained that five or six former members who had left the church because of a staff departure were criticizing him on social media. The staff member had been let go for moral failure, and Aaron, appropriately, had not shared all the details; but these former members refused to accept his explanation.

He looked away for a moment, gathering his thoughts. "The church has no authority over them," he said. "They're free to say awful things about me. I feel terrible for my family. My daughters, ages nine and eleven, hear about these posts at school. My church supports me and the tough decision we had to make, but these few people are making my life miserable."

Marcus is another pastor I coach. He leads a nondenominational church in northern California. When I asked how he was doing, he opened up quickly.

"Since you asked, I'll tell you," he said with a sad smile. "This morning began with three nastygrams: two emails and one anonymous letter. Usually, I don't get three of those in a month, so having them all in one morning was tough."

We talked briefly about the issues behind the negative correspondence, each unrelated to the others. Then he continued describing his day.

"Midmorning, after dealing with a few more routine items, I went to the hospital. One of my deacons is a close friend, and he's dying of cancer. He has three young kids. I'm torn up about it. I have to practice a lot of self-control not to cry when I'm with him. He's so courageous—he says he's ready to go, but I'm having trouble letting go."

After a deep breath, Marcus moved on to a more encouraging moment. "I've been meeting a businessman for coffee and lunch for almost three months. He's had a lot of questions about religion, faith, and Christ. But today, something clicked. It was like a light turned on when we talked about Jesus. I think he's close to becoming a believer. It was a real encouragement."

He then switched to his afternoon. "I set aside four hours for sermon prep, but I had three interruptions, so I got maybe two hours done. I'll have to stay up late tonight to catch up. I almost canceled our five o'clock session, but I really wanted to talk."

As we wrapped up our hour together, Marcus glanced at his phone.

"Ugh," he mumbled, then quickly recovered. "Sorry," he said, realizing we were still on our video call. "It's a note from my most vicious critic in the church. I have to deal with this now."

He looked directly into the Zoom camera. "This pastoring stuff is a roller coaster, isn't it? I don't know if I'll ever get used to the ups and downs."

The challenge for church members is to pray, and that includes praying for their pastors. Satan wants to destroy the local church, and one of his key targets is pastors.

When I was a pastor, Frances Mason organized an intercessory prayer ministry for me. Over one hundred church members prayed for me every day at noon—that's more than 35,000 prayers a year for me and my ministry. It was powerful. It changed my life and made a tremendous difference in my church.

Those one hundred or so men and women were asked to set aside just one minute a day to pray for me. Many chose noon as a simple reminder. Some prayed longer. A few prayed an hour a day.

I was humbled. I was grateful. I was blessed.

Here are a few examples of what they prayed for me daily:

- anointed sermons
- my family members, by name
- protection from discouragement
- protection from temptation
- discernment
- opportunities to share my faith
- my prayer commitment
- my leadership
- dealing with critics
- future direction for the church

- my physical health
- protection from burnout
- staff relations
- my marriage

Your local church is where you can make a difference—a place where you can live a life of significance. Perhaps one of the greatest contributions you can make is to pray for your church, and specifically for your pastor.

The power of prayer will transform your pastor.

The power of prayer will transform your church.

The power of prayer will transform you.

Start now. Pray for your pastor every day, even if it's only for one minute.

Pray for Other Church Members

I learned this approach from a woman named Evelyn, a member of a church my team consulted. She told me she prays for other church members ten minutes each day: five minutes to pray for five different church members, and five minutes to text or email each one to let them know she prayed for them.

That's it. Ten minutes.

Let me share the rest of the story.

We heard about Evelyn while doing a consultation at her church—a congregation that had recently turned around from decline to growth. When I asked the pastor why he needed a consultation, he said he wanted to maintain momentum. When I asked what had started the turnaround, he admitted he really didn't know.

During our interviews, many people mentioned Evelyn. She was already on our list, so I made sure to talk with her personally.

When she described her process of praying, texting, and emailing, I asked how she obtained members' contact information.

"I asked them," she said matter-of-factly. "I told them I wouldn't use it for any reason other than to pray for them. No one turned me down."

Shortly after Evelyn started her prayer ministry, two others joined her. The three divided the church membership among themselves, so each member was prayed for more often. Over time, more people joined the prayer effort. By the time of our consultation, eleven people were involved in the ministry, meaning fifty-five members were being prayed for every day. With 450 total members, each one was prayed for about forty-five times a year—nearly once a week.

That's prayer in action.

As we learned about Evelyn's ministry, we discovered that about seven months after she began praying, the church's decline halted. Four months later, it started growing for the first time in more than a decade. Can we prove cause and effect? No. Can we say prayer was likely instrumental? Absolutely.

Here are some direct comments we heard in interviews:

- "The whole attitude of the church got so much better once Evelyn's ministry started growing."
- "We were a complacent church until this prayer ministry came along."
- "Some members were surprised to see prayers being answered—it changed their attitude."
- "I can't remember the last time we had a church fight. I'm convinced it's because of Evelyn's prayer ministry."

Get the picture? Others joined the prayer ministry later, but it might have succeeded with Evelyn alone. That's the power of one faithful church member who's willing to pray.

You can be an Evelyn in your church. You don't have to replicate her exact ministry, but you can start somewhere. I'm convinced that prayer ministries of various shapes and sizes have been pivotal in many church turnarounds.

As a postscript, I want to mention Lillian Anderson, who went to heaven after contracting COVID-19. Lillian had a similar ministry to Evelyn's in a church I pastored in St. Petersburg in the late 1980s. That church had been in decline for years, but it began to turn around. Though several factors contributed, I'm convinced Lillian's prayers were God's primary instrument. When we reach heaven, I believe God will show us how men and women of prayer—people like

Lillian and Evelyn—were his chosen instruments to revitalize these churches.

Have I convinced you yet about the power of prayer for your church? It might be your time to become a Lillian or an Evelyn. Find a way to pray for your fellow church members. It's called radical prayer, but it's really the normal Christian life.

Pray for Workers in the Harvest

Earlier in the book, I shared my story of becoming a committed church member. For years, I preached in a different church almost every weekend. But then I made a commitment to stay in one place, to be a biblical church member. I love it. I love the rhythms of church life, seeing how one week's ministry builds on the next. And I love serving at the church where my son Jess is lead pastor.

For a few years, we've closed every worship service by reading Matthew 9:36-38 together:

> When he saw the crowds, he had compassion on them because they were confused and helpless, like sheep without a shepherd. He said to his disciples, "The harvest is great, but the workers are few. So pray to the Lord who is in charge of the harvest; ask him to send more workers into his fields."

Over time, as we continued reading these verses, I began to wonder if we should be more intentional about praying for workers in the harvest. Jesus is the Lord of the harvest fields. He commands us to pray for more workers.

Jesus has called and chosen us to share the gospel. The Great Commission passages in Matthew 28:18-20 and Acts 1:8 are clear indicators that we are to go and proclaim the Good News. Jesus also said he wants more followers to be his witnesses.

Do you see the essence of Matthew 9:36-38? Our challenge isn't finding more "prospects" for our churches; our challenge is finding more workers to go to them.

One of the most powerful ways to live a life of significance is to obey Matthew 9:36-38. You can be part of God's plan to see people come to Christ. Your ministry in your church should include praying regularly and faithfully for more workers to go into the harvest.

If even a few church members would pray such prayers consistently, I believe our churches would see new signs of life and hope.

Will you pray for workers in the harvest fields? Will you pray regularly and faithfully to that end?

Pray for Your Church's Ministries

Whenever I see a church ministry making a difference—reaching people and discipling them—I typically find prayer at its foundation. Let's consider one example.

Faith Presbyterian Church had a small-group ministry called life groups, which had produced significant fruit over the years. Members who joined a life group tended to be more committed to the church. They invited others more often, read their Bibles daily, and participated in the church's other ministries. They also gave more generously.

On the topic of giving, the financial assistant did a study and found that life group members gave twelve times more per capita than those who weren't in a group. The difference was striking.

In recent years, though, the life groups had struggled. The church previously started at least one new life group each year, but members were now unwilling to leave their current groups to start a new one. Attendance declined, and giving followed suit.

Someone suggested featuring a different life group on the church website each week and recognizing that group in Sunday worship. Each Sunday, church members were asked to pray for the individuals in the featured group. Eventually, those group members would stand up so the congregation could see the people they were praying for. With eleven adult life groups, each one received focused prayer once a quarter.

The results were positive and obvious. Attendance grew and giving increased. Within a year, three new life groups started—a milestone that had happened only once before in the church's history.

The point is simple yet profound. Most churches have multiple ministries and programs, but how often do members pray for them consistently? Do you see your prayer ministry as one that includes praying for your church's programs and ministries? Think of the profound impact such prayers could have.

Here's another example. The 2020 pandemic prompted many churches to expand their digital ministries. Some churches, unsure what to do with online viewers, simply let them watch anonymously. Others saw these virtual attendees as a God-given opportunity. One church in Michigan provided a link for prayer requests during and after their streamed worship services. The response started slowly but then grew steadily. Though digital viewing decreased over time, the number of prayer requests did not. A Muslim man in Indonesia even contacted the church weekly for prayer.

Months after the quarantine ended, four families whose first contact was through the online prayer ministry joined the church in person. God might be calling you to a ministry of prayer for digital participants. If your church already has one, you could join it. If not, maybe you're called to start it. The impact could be huge—another step toward a life of significance.

Pray for Your Community

A church in Georgia created a digital map of all the streets and house numbers within a ten-minute drive of the building—about three thousand homes in total. The facilities manager posted this map in the foyer. Ten church members each volunteered to pray for ten homes a day, covering one hundred homes daily. The goal was to pray for every home in a month.

They planned to continue for six months, with a different monthly focus: salvation, marriages, children, grief, addictions, and openness to an invitation to church.

This church's average attendance was only about fifty, so they didn't have a large pool of resources or volunteers. But they were committed to prayer. They prayed consistently for those six months. Although they hadn't explicitly aimed to grow, the congregation increased from fifty to seventy-five within a year, and the members were excited by how visibly prayer was making a difference.

After taking a three-month break, they've begun the prayer ministry again. As I write, phase two is underway. I won't be surprised if they continue to see God's blessings.

The Hope Initiative (see HopeInitiative.com) is a similar ministry, in which church members pray for their community by walking through neighborhoods and praying in front of each home, optionally leaving a door hanger to let residents know they were prayed for.

The possibilities for praying for your community are endless. You can ask local leaders how to pray for them, send notes to schoolteachers letting them know you're praying, or find creative ways to engage merchants in prayer. A healthy church loves its community—and prays for it.

Where to Begin?

The ways you can pray for your church are many. You likely can't do all of them at once, so where should you start?

First, pray for direction. God might open doors you don't expect. In other words, pray about prayer.

Second, follow your passion. Has something in this chapter stirred your heart? Could you be excited about one of these ideas or about another approach you have in mind?

Third, if you're still unsure, consider starting by praying for your pastor. I interact daily with hurting pastors who need our prayers. Look at my book *When the People Pray*. It is a thirty-day guide to pray for your pastor. A healthy church rarely exists with an emotionally or spiritually unhealthy pastor.

There is no such thing as a life of significance without a life of prayer. God has placed you in your church for such a time as this, so that you can be an instrument of prayer. Scripture is full of commands for believers to pray. For example, Paul exhorts the church at Rome, "Rejoice in our confident hope. Be patient in trouble, and keep on praying" (Romans 12:12).

"Keep on praying." That was God's mandate to the Roman believers two thousand years ago. It's our mandate today.

And it's a crucial commitment for radical Christians who are radical church members.

Three Questions

1. Why is praying for ourselves necessary for a vibrant prayer ministry as church members?
2. If you were to design a prayer ministry to pray for all the members of your church, what would it look like?
3. What are some reasons it's so important to pray for our pastors?

6

That Attendance Thing

Alex had not attended church in three weeks.

In many churches today, a relatively short period of absence is considered no big deal. Three weeks away could be an extended vacation or a long business trip. Alex's absence might not even be noticed in many churches today.

But this was in 1993, not today. Though I'm not advocating a return to yesteryear or longing for the good old days, there were different expectations in most churches back then. Alex's absence caught a lot of people's attention.

Alex was a thirtysomething divorced man with no immediate family in town. He was very active in our church. With few exceptions, he attended Sunday worship services, participated in his Bible study group every week, and served faithfully in ministry. In almost every way, he was an ideal church member.

It was not like Alex to be gone for two weeks, much less three. The good news was that we noticed his absence. Though we didn't track individual worship attendance, we did record everyone who attended a Bible study group. Alex had missed three weeks in a row.

The study groups had both a personal and a systematic approach to ministry. The systematic approach included a "missed you" card for every person absent on a given Sunday. That card was promptly mailed to Alex the Monday after his first absence.

At the two-week mark, absentees received a phone call. Several class members were worried about Alex and tried calling him. There was no answer. In 1993, cell phones were not ubiquitous, and many people did not have voicemail (though some had answering machines). It wasn't unusual to not be able to reach someone if they were out of town.

Indeed, that was our assumption about Alex. He worked in industrial sales, traveled frequently, and was typically careful to return in time for church. We assumed he might be on an extended business trip. We decided to wait one more Sunday.

When Alex didn't show up for a third Sunday, his class was on full alert. The card and calls had not reached him, so it was time to visit his home.

Three men—close friends of Alex—drove the short distance. Each had tried calling him and was surprised he hadn't responded. Something was clearly off.

They knocked but received no answer. They tried louder knocks and rang the doorbell multiple times. Finally, Alex opened the door. What they saw shocked them.

He was still in his pajamas on a Sunday afternoon. He obviously hadn't shaved for weeks. His eyes were red and swollen, and he smelled as if he hadn't bathed or showered in some time.

His friends had never seen Alex looking disheveled. He was usually meticulous about his appearance. Something was definitely wrong.

They finally got Alex to talk. He shared his story. A little over three weeks ago, his mother had died. He had been very close to her—she was his rock during his divorce. Her death sent him into a deep depression. He called in sick for a week, then took two weeks of vacation.

His friends asked him about his plans for the following week. He answered, with little emotion, "I was thinking of killing myself."

The men began getting Alex both medical and psychological help. Though it wasn't easy, he gradually emerged from his depression and was eventually able to resume a more normal life. His friends had literally saved his life. Indeed, his church had saved his life.

Though Alex's story isn't typical, it's not entirely out of the norm either. People are hurting. The apostle Paul reminds us that members of the church are to care for one another.

> This makes for harmony among the members, so that all the members care for each other. If one part suffers, all the parts suffer with it, and if one part is honored, all the parts are glad.
>
> **1 CORINTHIANS 12:25-26**

Our church had specific trigger points to prompt us to reach out to members. Some of those triggers related directly to attendance. We knew something was wrong if a member's attendance pattern changed.

Again, I'm not trying to recover or revere the past. Instead, I want to remind church leaders and members that attendance is important for many reasons, including the ministry reason demonstrated by Alex's experience.

In the rest of this chapter, we'll explore other reasons why faithful attendance is crucial for churches. We'll also show that expecting faithful attendance is neither legalistic nor unbiblical. Church members should be expected to attend. Church members should be expected to gather. Indeed, that's the essence of the original term used for the church.

Ekklesia

In the city-states of ancient Greece, *ekklesia* described an assembly of citizens. The word literally means "called-out ones." People were called out of their homes and the marketplace to assemble and conduct major civic business—they were called out to gather.

Ekklesia is the most common word for the church in the New Testament. Like their secular counterparts, church members were called out to gather. Don't miss that meaning: The church was expected to gather.

What does this word teach us today? First, *ekklesia* clearly refers to people, not buildings. When some say the church is the people, not the building, they're correct. Second, don't ignore the full weight of the word. The *ekklesia* are called out of their homes and families to gather with their church family. The term doesn't specify the type of facility or location; instead, it focuses on the *gathering*.

We noted that in ancient Greece, the *ekklesia* was a solemn and serious meeting to handle important governmental and societal matters. It was among the most significant assemblies of its day.

When the church adopted *ekklesia*, they embraced a similar intention. The *ekklesia* was an important gathering for important matters. According to Acts 2:42-47, those matters included listening to the apostles' teaching, enjoying fellowship, sharing meals, praying, giving of their finances, and worshiping together.

Do you see the picture? The church is meant to gather. The church is mandated to gather. Simply stated, you can't have a life of purpose if you are not regularly gathering with fellow believers in your church.

Why do some believers resist faithful gathering today? Though we lack definitive data, two movements seem to push back on this concept:

1. It has become fashionable to emphasize that "the church is the people, not the building," implying that meeting at a building isn't as vital as individual expressions of faith. This view can become overly individualistic. The church is both gathered and scattered. Neither aspect should be minimized.
2. Some dislike the word *attendance* as a synonym for gathering, possibly seeing it as legalistic or compulsory. Even if we used a different term, most people will continue to talk about "attending" church.

Ekklesia connotes a gathering for an important purpose. In ancient Greece, the purpose was civic. For the New Testament church, the purpose was to encourage and equip believers, to give, and to serve. Both were vital gatherings in their context. But the New Testament gathering is infinitely more significant: the business of the Kingdom of God.

What is the link between the gathered church and the scattered church? The *ekklesia* is indeed both. The gathered church was never meant to remain inwardly focused; it was meant to go and make disciples. The early church learned this lesson the hard way: they stayed in Jerusalem despite Christ's words in Acts 1:8 until persecution came in Acts 8:1.

When Gathered Becomes Scattered

Limesdale Community Church has a relatively brief but rich history, now nearing thirty years. For most of that time, it included its denominational name, which was replaced with Community about a decade ago. The Limesdale neighborhood has nearly four hundred homes in a town of fifteen thousand residents. For years, it was the place of choice for young, middle-class families.

The local school system attracted many of those families. Its elementary and middle schools had some of the highest test scores in the state.

The church grew alongside the community, and many families formed close connections. Growth was steady, and assimilation was high.

Then the community changed—initially in subtle ways. No one can pinpoint exactly when. Perhaps it started when the first generation's children finished middle school and families moved closer to other high schools. Maybe it was economic: The homes were no longer new, and many owners moved on, causing property values to drop. The lower prices attracted a slightly less affluent demographic. The church, in turn, became more of a commuter congregation, as many longtime members continued attending despite moving out of the neighborhood.

The pastor of Limesdale Community Church contacted our team at Church Answers. His concern was simple: The church was no longer growing. In fact, attendance had declined 12 percent over five years—an average of less than 3 percent a year, barely noticeable to most. Yet the leaders sensed something was amiss. They'd never experienced a sustained decline and viewed their church as a model for outreach and ministry.

No more.

During my first debriefing with the leadership, an eager elder asked, "So, what's wrong with our church?"

I answered succinctly, "You are not growing because you are not reaching your community."

Stunned silence followed, more disappointed than shocked. They'd expected something more profound.

The pastor broke in, "So, what do we do?"

Again, I was direct: "Start reaching your community."

I explained that Limesdale's growth had once been easy because members largely lived in the neighborhood. Relationships came naturally, and people regularly invited neighbors to church. Over time, however, the neighborhood changed and the church didn't. To grow again, they had to engage the current residents. As those residents connected, they would naturally invite their neighbors.

An elder responded and perhaps unintentionally revealed a deeper issue. "But that would mean giving up our church to people we don't know."

Ouch.

Whether he realized it or not, he admitted they saw the church as "our church," focusing on control rather than reaching new people. Our consulting team didn't give them the answer they wanted. They desired growth, but not if it involved people different from them. Two years later, the church's slow decline continued. COVID-19 accelerated it, and the church is now in danger of closing.

This situation contrasts sharply with the first church in Jerusalem, which exploded with growth after Christ commanded them to reach the world (Acts 1:8). Acts 2:47 captures the momentum: "Each day the Lord added to their fellowship those who were being saved."

At first glance, the Jerusalem church and Limesdale have nothing in common—one vibrant, one dying. But both failed to fully obey the Great Commission. The Jerusalem church initially stayed in Jerusalem rather than moving on to Judea, Samaria, and beyond (Acts 1:8). Limesdale ceased any noticeable outreach at all.

As noted, the Jerusalem church needed persecution (Acts 8:1) to push them beyond their comfort zone.

What does this have to do with attendance? The *ekklesia* exists to gather and then scatter. If a congregation disobeys this twofold mandate—gathering and going—it becomes inwardly focused, loses its purpose, and ultimately forfeits its reason for being.

Attendance dwindles when the scattering stops. A healthy gathering church and a healthy scattering church go hand in hand.

If you sense your own commitment slipping, it might be because your church has become inwardly focused. Or perhaps you have.

Slipping Away

Attendance matters. It's a commitment to be present, an indicator that your actions align with your words. Attendance isn't a legalistic rule. It simply means you're truly dedicated.

I recently spoke with a man whose thirty-year marriage ended. He explained it wasn't a sudden event but a gradual erosion, day by day. No dramatic betrayal—just a slow fade until they realized they were merely roommates.

Likewise, many church members drift away gradually. When COVID hit, it offered a convenient exit for those whose commitment was already waning. Some briefly watched online, but many dropped out altogether. The marginally churched became the unchurched.

We've rightly focused on how this massive dropout has hurt churches, but we've overlooked its effect on the individuals who left. The New Testament teaches that a life of significance is found in Christ, and Christ designed us to serve and give within the local church. Abandoning active participation in the church means forfeiting a life of purpose. Without active involvement, uncommitted Christians lose fellowship, accountability, and the shared ministry described by Paul in 1 Corinthians.

Living a life of significance means living for Christ and others with a sacrificial attitude. Otherwise, our lives can slide into self-focus and diminished impact.

What are some signs someone is slipping away?

Becoming Critical of the Pastor and Others

No church is perfect, and there will always be something to criticize. An early warning sign is when you focus on problems more than on solutions. You might judge sermons instead of seeking God's voice. You might complain about music, service length, or ministry programs.

You become a critic rather than a worshiper, encourager, servant, or generous giver. In Matthew 7:5, Jesus warns about seeing the speck in someone else's eye while missing the log in your own. A critical spirit damages relationships—whether in friendship, marriage, business, or the church.

Distancing Ourselves from Others in the Church

Think about the close relationships you once had. Maybe they were in a prayer group, a small group, or a ministry team. Now you notice fewer connections. Perhaps people have tried contacting you, but you haven't responded. Or maybe no one has followed up, and you feel justified in slipping away because they didn't notice or reach out.

You once took the initiative to stay connected and help others stay connected. Now you're the one drifting. You can see where it's leading—you may soon become a church dropout.

Becoming a Worship-Only Attender

For years, you attended worship as well as a small group or Sunday school class, and served in a ministry. Now you only attend the worship service. What's wrong with that?

A few years ago, our Church Answers team researched assimilation, the likelihood that someone will remain at a church long-term. One key finding was that those who regularly attend both worship and a small group are five times more likely to stick with their church than those who attend worship only. In other words, involvement in at least two areas significantly increases staying power.

Worship attendance is great—you hear God's Word, sing praises, and share a communal experience. But if that's all you do, you're less likely to remain. You may not be building the relationships or serving in ways that create a "stickiness." Over time, you're more apt to fade away.

Focusing on Our Own Preferences

Everyone in a church should receive ministry. The body of Christ is designed to meet needs. Preferences, however, are different from needs. Preferences focus on oneself rather than on others. You might fixate on a particular worship style, order of service, or building amenities. Once you get those preferences met, you'll likely find something else to be dissatisfied with. Preferences are never fully satisfied.

God designed the church to be others-focused, not preference-focused. First Corinthians 12:25 says we are to care for one another. Then in 1 Corinthians 13, Paul emphasizes that even if we have great knowledge, faith, and sacrificial giving, if we don't love one another, we gain nothing. This love doesn't demand its own way (1 Corinthians 13:5). Healthy church members look out for others, not themselves.

Do any of these indicators describe you? Maybe you've already dropped out. Recognizing these signs may explain how it happened. Perhaps God is nudging you to return. The local church is where God will use you most fully and where you'll discover a life of significance.

Attendance Is for Rebels

If you faithfully attend your church, you stand out in today's culture. You might even be a true rebel.

Decades ago, attendance sometimes had a legalistic feel. Churchgoing was culturally expected. Some, like certain politicians I've known, attended sporadically but showed up more often during election season to gain support. They used the church for their own ends.

Times have changed. Today, regular churchgoers are a distinct minority. It's countercultural to attend church, and society generally accepts nonattendance.

Yet consider how the early Christians—imperfect, opposed, and in the minority—still changed the world. By Christ's power, they turned the world upside down.

A life of significance is realized only through Christ's power at work in you, and that life is meant to be lived in active involvement in a local church. So does church attendance matter?

Yes, it does.

It can change the world.

It's a crucial commitment.

Three Questions

1. How does *ekklesia* imply that churches should both gather and scatter?
2. What are some of the most common reasons you've seen for active church members to become less active or inactive?
3. How are 1 Corinthians 12 and 1 Corinthians 13 connected to church membership?

7

"Community" Is Not Just a Buzzword

Everyone needs a Dan in their lives, at least for a season.

I was pastoring a church in Florida when Dan dropped into my life. He showed up at the church asking for three things: food, a place to stay for one night, and information on how to become a Christian.

Yes, I was a bit excited about the third request.

Dan not only became a Christian, he became one of the most dedicated followers of Christ I have ever known. Prior to our meeting, he had never been inside a church building. Indeed, he asked countless questions about why we did what we did in our church. He stretched me with those questions—sometimes I had to concede there was really no good reason for certain things we did.

If Dan had a downside, it was his seeming inability to filter what came out of his mouth. It was problematic at first because his vocabulary was filled with profanity. But Dan was teachable. If I told him a word was unacceptable, he never used it again. In fact, he once made an appointment just so I could teach him which words he shouldn't say. I've never had a pastoral counseling session quite like that one.

The filtering problem rose again when he mentioned to several church members that he had spent an hour with me learning cusswords.

Dan was indeed a challenge, but a blessed challenge. I would take a dozen Dans, with his unbridled enthusiasm, in any church.

But let's return to the first day I met Dan, when he asked for those three things. After I told him how he could become a Christian, he quickly repented of his sin and placed his faith in Christ. I was overjoyed, but unprepared for his next question: "What do I do now?"

Up to this point, most new Christians I knew already attended church. They heard the gospel from the pulpit, in a small group, or from a fellow member. They naturally discerned the next steps. They didn't need to ask "What do I do now?" because they were already connected.

Dan didn't know the rules. He knew nothing about church.

My response was to point him toward the same path I

recommend for other new believers: *Get involved in a local church*. I also told him he needed to study the Bible on his own. I gave him a new Bible and a copy of *What the Bible Is All About*, by Henrietta Mears, and I spent some time teaching him about prayer.

But no matter what you've heard, I did not teach him any cusswords.

Perhaps the most important recommendation I gave him at the time was to get into a group. If I had told Dan he "needed community," he probably would have looked at me with that quizzical expression he often had. That cliché phrase would have meant nothing to him. Instead, I told him he needed to join a group.

Groups have a plethora of names: community groups, life groups, home groups, Sunday school classes, Bible study groups, connect groups, cell groups, fellowship groups, and others. At the time, our primary groups were called Sunday school classes.

Because our church had never welcomed a new Christian quite like Dan, I was careful where I sent him. I asked him to check out a men's group, an eclectic collection of guys with a variety of backgrounds and experiences. They welcomed Dan, eccentricities and all, and he thrived in their Sunday school class.

He also stopped cussing.

I often wonder what I would have done if I couldn't point

Dan to a local church. Sometimes we take the local church for granted. In the United States alone, there are around 350,000 churches,[5] and it's easy to think of them as commodities rather than the precious expressions of Christ's body that they are.

I wonder what I would have done if I didn't have a group to recommend to Dan.

When Dan got involved in Sunday school, his rough edges actually refined many of our members. They walked alongside him, helping him grow as a believer. Dan asked questions—including many questions we hadn't anticipated—forcing us to think deeply and turn to the Bible for answers.

I saw the body of Christ emerge in the harmony between Dan and the other church members. Each member cared for the others. Members used their gifts as God intended. Of course, our humanity and sin sometimes got in the way, but overall the body of Christ functioned well.

Now, let's think about how Dan's story relates to yours.

Groups: A Critical Commitment

Let me remind you we are not going through a legalistic checklist of commitments. We are observing the healthiest church members and the types of commitments they have made. Healthy church members make healthy churches.

The first crucial commitment was radical prayer.

The second crucial commitment was faithful attendance.

And now, we look at the third crucial commitment that shapes healthy church members. Simply stated, it's involvement in a small group in the church.

Like Dan, you must become deeply connected with a church to make a difference. A life of significance doesn't happen in isolation; it happens in community. Yep, there's that word again.

So what does community look like? How do we turn the theory of connection into practice? The answers aren't earthshaking—more reminders than revelation—but they're important nonetheless.

The Fellowship Factor

"Fellowship" can be vague. It might mean camaraderie, a shared interest, or simply an association. In church culture, it can also refer to a potluck supper.

In the Bible, the Greek word most often used for fellowship is *koinonia*, found nineteen times in the New Testament. It may also be translated "contribution," "participation," or "sharing." At its heart, *koinonia* refers to intimate participation in a gathering where the participants care deeply for one another.

When you attend church or otherwise connect with a congregation, your actions say you care about others. Unlike a potluck, where your biggest hope might be someone bringing banana pudding, your motive in *koinonia* is to do for others, serve others, and give to others.

Koinonia is especially powerful in groups.

Fellowship is as much an attitude as it is an action. Certainly, action is necessary, but it's driven by a joyful, giving spirit.

Some years ago, I decided to start acting like a church member. For many years, I'd served as an interim pastor or accepted preaching invitations, and I was gone from my home church almost every Sunday. Then God convicted me to attend and serve in my own church weekly.

It was one of the best decisions of my life. Nellie Jo and I got involved by joining a small group and discipling friends in the church. We even took on janitorial duties—taking out trash and cleaning toilets.

God used these roles to remind me of what it means to be part of Christ's body. I was the real beneficiary, receiving far more than I gave.

When the pandemic arrived in 2020, I missed my church involvement terribly. Yes, I joined online services and Zoom meetings, but digital platforms aren't true fellowship. I wasn't able to serve others like before. I was receiving more than giving.

By the way, I occasionally get to preach in my home church, where one of my sons is the pastor. But my wife strongly prefers his preaching, so my time in the pulpit is limited.

That's okay. I still have fellowship, particularly in my community group.

The Discipleship Issue

If *fellowship* can be ambiguous, *discipleship* can be downright confusing.

For some, discipleship is about information and knowledge—learning more about Christ and the Bible. For others, it's almost synonymous with mentoring—one person guiding another. In some churches, discipleship might be tied to a specific program or meeting time.

In general, discipleship means we're becoming more like Jesus. A life of significance is a life of discipleship—becoming more like Christ. There's no other path to the abundant, purposeful life.

I wonder what Jesus' first followers thought as he ascended into heaven. Two men in white, presumably angels, asked them, "Why are you standing here staring into heaven?" (Acts 1:11).

Jesus had told them not to leave Jerusalem until the Holy Spirit came (Acts 1:4). So they waited—together. Jesus could have sent the Spirit to each one individually, but he wanted them together. He wanted them to start a church, not move on their own.

Jesus wanted them to become more like him as they served one another in a local church. Thus, the first church—Jerusalem—was founded.

What did this church do? Acts 2:42 says, "All the believers devoted themselves to the apostles' teaching, and to fellowship, and to sharing in meals (including the Lord's Supper), and to prayer."

They gathered. They learned from the apostles. They practiced selfless fellowship, shared meals (including the Lord's Supper), and devoted themselves to prayer.

It's abundantly clear that Jesus intended for his followers to become more like him through serving in a local congregation. Initially, they gathered before they scattered.

The same lesson applies today. You will become more like Jesus as you serve him through a local church. And you will especially grow as a disciple in a group. While you'll practice some spiritual disciplines on your own, most of your growth as a disciple will occur in the context of your church, and particularly in a group.

A life of significance is a life of discipleship—of becoming more like Jesus. That life won't fully blossom outside the local church. But it will blossom fully in a group.

The Power of Relationships

We're designed to be connected to a local church. We're saved by Christ to become part of his body here on earth.

Relationships overlap with both fellowship and discipleship. Through fellowship, we serve sacrificially. Through discipleship, we become more like Jesus. Both thrive through healthy relationships.

I recently learned again the power of a group when Nellie Jo and I joined a cross-generational group we call Pericope. Though the other members are younger than we are, Nellie Jo and I love doing life with them. The members of Pericope have become dear friends. I can't imagine growing as a Christian without the relationships, prayer support, and accountability of my community group.

The members of our community group grasp the incredible power of relationships. They find significance in the church through connecting both with church members and with those outside. I've personally been encouraged by them on many occasions—sometimes they had no idea I was struggling, yet their words lifted me.

I've watched them interact with other members as well—always consistent, engaging, and joyful. Yet they don't see themselves as doing anything special. They're simply reflecting Christ's presence in their lives, naturally and supernaturally.

Their focus isn't merely inward. They also invite guests and reach out to people who rarely attend church. They're quick to greet those who feel out of place, making them feel comfortable.

The members of our group are living lives of significance. Only eternity will reveal the full impact they've had—how many hearts they've lifted, how many people they've guided toward Jesus. And they do it through their local church. They're wholly committed church members.

If you suggested they could find a life of purpose outside the church and outside our community group, I suspect they'd either stare at you blankly or strongly disagree. They get it. They understand the value of group-based relationships, and they practice it in their local congregation.

They are living lives of significance.

What's Next?

Perhaps you're convinced by now. Maybe you fully agree that church members should connect through fellowship, discipleship, and relationships. Perhaps you grasp the incredible power of connecting with a group in your church. Yet, like Dan, you might be wondering, "What do I do now?"

We insist a life of significance means being involved and connected in a local church through fellowship, discipleship, and relationships. But we need practical steps or it remains mere theory.

There's a risk of being too prescriptive. First, a checklist can become legalistic. If you're active in church for the wrong reasons, you'll burn out or drop out. Second, every church is different, so we need to contextualize.

Our biblical solution lies in Acts 2:42-47, a powerful example from the first church. Though there are other passages, this one is especially relevant as it describes the earliest Christians.

We can identify five steps to move us toward a life of

significance: praying together, worshiping together, gathering in small groups, doing the work of ministry together, and giving generously.

But here is the added value: Our community group is a constant and positive reminder that these five steps are crucial commitments.

Worship Together

At different times in this book, I've pointed to the need for committed Christians to "attend church," or to be faithful attenders of worship services. Here's where groups and worship attendance merge. Those who are in groups are also likely to be faithful worship attenders.

One common way we express our connection to a local church is by saying, "I attend church at Faithview Community." Attendance denotes the gathered church, and the gathered church matters. As noted in the previous chapter, worship attendance is a true spiritual discipline.

In Acts 2:46, the early believers "worshiped together at the Temple each day." Only a few weeks had passed since Jesus' crucifixion, resurrection, and ascension, so these new believers gathered regularly to worship their risen Lord. They remembered his death through the Lord's Supper (Acts 2:42), celebrated his resurrection in gathered worship (Acts 2:44), witnessed the Spirit's power among them (Acts 2:43), and practiced generous giving (Acts 2:45).

Notice the theme: They remembered and celebrated together. They saw God's power together. They encouraged one another together. They gave abundantly together.

In our community group, we remind each other every week of the power of gathering and worshiping together. We keep each other accountable for attending services. Some of us compare sermon notes from the previous Sunday.

Today's culture often downplays the importance of believers gathering. Attending worship can be seen as just one choice among many. But if you want to overcome that cultural headwind, you must commit—without reservation—to make weekly worship central in your life. It's vital for living a life of significance.

It's what committed church members do.

Practically, this means worship attendance isn't just another activity. You don't skip it for sports, recreation, or sleeping in. You don't replace in-person worship with digital viewing unless absolutely necessary. A life of significance is forged by following Jesus Christ, both personally and through the local church.

Society may find it strange. They may label you a fanatic. The early Christians were similarly misunderstood, but they remained faithful to gather. They became history's greatest difference makers. That's our path too.

Gather Small

I recall the offering envelope checkoff system from my younger years. If you're not familiar with it, let me reminisce briefly.

When I was young, we put our offering in an envelope for the plate. On that envelope was a list of disciplines, which we'd check off if we'd done them:

- Sunday School Attendance
- Bible Brought
- Bible Read Daily
- Lesson Studied
- Giving
- Worship Attendance

Some envelopes just said "Present" for the first line, implying you weren't really present unless you attended Sunday school. At the heart of that system was the principle that one of the most important acts of faithfulness was belonging to a small group.

Though the checkoff system is largely gone (and online giving is making offering envelopes obsolete), I sometimes miss the reminders. They prompted us to be active in a small group and in worship, to give faithfully, and to read our Bibles daily.

Acts 2:46 shows that the early church moved from larger to smaller gatherings: "They worshiped together at the Temple each day, met in homes for the Lord's Supper, and shared their meals with great joy and generosity."

A life of significance is tied to other believers in the church. We can't make a real difference if we're alone. Small groups are where we connect to do ministry, invite others, hold each other accountable, and find purpose.

Do the Work of Ministry Together

I once spoke with a pastor in North Carolina who led a remarkable rural church. The town's population was barely over 200, yet the church averaged nearly 250 in worship. Incredible.

During our conversation, he shared an email from the town's mayor that best explained the church's success. With minor edits, here's what the mayor wrote:

> Pastor,
>
> I've lived here all my life and I've never seen anything like your church. We're not a wealthy community, but any time we face a challenge, someone from your church is right there. It's remarkable.
>
> I've never thought much about religion, but watching your church has me reconsidering. You

helped after the tornado, you run an incredible after-school program, and you partnered with us to care for seniors.

I could go on. Your church is a ministry machine. Please don't stop being so active. I've never seen anything like it, especially from a church. I'm so grateful.

Your friend,

I love that phrase "ministry machine." The mayor understands how Christians working together in the local church can accomplish more than individuals alone. He's amazed by the people serving. And that's the point. The church is not just an organization; it's believers united in ministry.

Here is what I love about that church in North Carolina. Most of their ministry emanates from their small groups. It's just what they do,

Yes, Christians can and should do ministry outside church. But when the body of Christ works together, the impact is far greater than the sum of the parts.

God put you on earth for two primary purposes. The first, often called the Great Commandment, is to love God and love others. The second, known as the Great Commission, is to go and make disciples. If you want a life of significance, fulfill these purposes in the context of your local church—loving God, loving others, and making disciples together. You're not just a spectator. You're an active participant in the ministry of Jesus.

Making a difference, now and eternally, is the life of a committed church member. We will unpack the commitment of doing ministry together in the next chapter.

Give Generously

Jesus spoke frequently about money. He said our hearts follow whatever we treasure (Matthew 6:21), and we cannot serve God and money (Matthew 6:24). These words are direct and convicting. If we don't hold our finances with open hands, we can't fully serve God and others.

My son Art, in his book *The Money Challenge*, emphasizes three perspectives: give generously, save wisely, and live appropriately. That's the open-handed approach Jesus taught. We must be willing—even eager—to give away our money. We must be prudent in saving for expected and unexpected needs. And we should live in humility and simplicity.

A life of significance is a life of overflowing generosity. And when believers in a local church combine their generosity, the effect is exponential. Such stewardship can truly change the world.

Money is simply a tool for generosity. We're to live with open hands, letting God's resources flow through us. The local church is the channel through which God desires to pour out his generosity.

Again, I mention this commitment in the context of a chapter on groups because group settings are where generosity abounds in most churches. When our team at Church Answers consults with a church, we sometimes ask them for a specific metric. We ask them to provide, without names, the median giving of church members in groups compared to members who are not in groups. *With consistency, those in groups give five to eight times more than those not in groups.*

Wow!

We will look at the commitment of generosity more deeply in the next chapter.

Give generously. It's a crucial commitment.

More Than a Cliché

At the beginning of this chapter, I told you about Dan, whose life was transformed by meeting Jesus and joining a local church. I shared how his life was transformed more deeply when he joined a Sunday school class.

Many in the church invested in Dan, but he gave back more than he received. Though he was unemployed at first, he found a job within days—grueling work in Florida's heat. Yet he still managed to join multiple church ministries. It was inspiring to watch him grow spiritually as he served other members, people in the community, and on missions trips.

Dan often expressed gratitude for our church. He also engaged in ministries beyond our church, but his greatest joy came from serving in the local congregation. He loved the fellowship, the sense of working together, and the accountability.

He loved his Sunday school class.

Dan's life was a life of significance—a life of commitment—a life of crucial commitments.

One of those crucial commitments was connecting with a small group or Sunday school class in the church.

That's the point of this book and the point made throughout the New Testament. The local church is God's plan A for difference-making disciples, and there is no plan B.

And small groups are a critical part of the journey.

Three Questions

1. What does "community" mean in the context of a local church?
2. Why should a small group or a Sunday school class be more than just another church activity? How does it become a crucial commitment to a believer?
3. Why do you think generosity is greater among group members in a church compared to those who attend worship only?

8

Simple Giving

Several years ago, Eric Geiger and I wrote a bestselling book called *Simple Church*. The thesis of the book was that church leaders should design a process of discipleship that is clear and actionable for church members. Those who come into the church should be able to understand clearly what options and actions they can take to become more like Christ.

Since the book was broad in its discipleship theme, we did not delve into specific areas such as giving and stewardship. But when I look back on my own journey on giving, I realize that I could have used a simple guideline to follow Jesus' examples on giving.

Since I had been out of church all of my teenager years, I was clueless about church life in general and giving in particular. I was then a young adult with a child on the way.

For sure, I knew what the offering plate was. And I knew that I was supposed to put a financial gift in the plate. But sadly, that was the extent of my stewardship knowledge. Eventually, I would develop my own simple giving plan. There was nothing original or unique about it, but it has served me well for four decades.

My plan for simple giving had the following five elements. Since my wife and I have all joint accounts and make financial decisions as one, it is really *our* plan instead of *my* plan.

1. The tithe is our minimum level of giving. I used the Old Testament tithe as my starting point. I don't worry about the debates on what you should tithe. We give 10 percent of our gross income as a starting point.
2. All of our tithe goes to our local church.
3. We ask God to keep us sensitive to giving beyond the tithe. Most of it is for increased giving in our church, but some of it goes beyond our local congregation.
4. Though we are not reckless, we try not to look at our income as our sole basis for giving. If we see a need, we might give beyond our income and trust God to provide.
5. We ask God to make us joyous givers. He has answered that prayer many times in our lives.

Our plan is descriptive of how God has led us. It is not necessarily prescriptive for others. I will say, however, that God has blessed us far beyond anything we could have imagined.

Simple giving is not just a financial act; it is a lifestyle of total commitment to following Jesus' teachings. In a world that prizes accumulation and self-interest, embracing a biblical perspective on generosity challenges us to a higher standard—a calling to give freely, joyfully, and sacrificially.

In basic terms, it is a crucial commitment.

Understanding Simple Giving

At its core, simple giving is about surrendering our lives to the will of God and placing our trust in him above all else. It requires us to move beyond mere tithing or a nominal act of charity and to see every gift—whether time, talent, or treasure—as a sacred opportunity to honor God and serve others. Simple giving is rooted in a profound understanding that all we have belongs to God, and our response should be a continual outpouring of faith expressed through generous deeds.

Jesus taught that generosity is a central mark of discipleship. In Matthew 6:19-21, he admonishes, "Don't store up treasures here on earth. . . . Store your treasures in heaven." This teaching calls us to reorient our hearts toward eternal values rather than transient earthly wealth. Simple giving is a tangible expression of this reorientation—it's a declaration that our ultimate security and hope are found not in material possessions but in our relationship with God.

Because the Bible Tells Me So

The Bible is replete with examples of simple generosity that challenge us to live beyond the conventional confines of self-interest. The early church in Acts 4:32-35 provides a powerful model of communal generosity, where believers shared everything in common, ensuring that "there were no needy people among them." Their simple giving was not motivated by compulsion, but by the love and unity that flowed from their shared commitment to Christ to live for him in the context of a local church.

Did you catch that? The first church in the Bible focused on giving and providing for others from the very beginning. The members of the early church made giving a crucial commitment.

Another profound example is the story of the widow's offering in Mark 12:41-44. Jesus observed a poor widow who put two very small copper coins into the Temple treasury. Although the amount was meager, Jesus recognized that she gave out of her poverty—everything she had to live on.

This act of simple giving, measured not by the value of the gift but by the depth of her sacrifice, teaches us that true generosity is defined by the heart rather than the sum. It challenges us to consider what it means to give sacrificially in a world where many cling tightly to what they have.

The apostle Paul also emphasizes the call to simple generosity in his letters. In 2 Corinthians 9:6-7, he reminds us that "the one who plants generously will get a generous crop." Paul encourages believers to give cheerfully, not reluctantly or under compulsion, highlighting that our giving is a response to the grace we have received through Christ. It is both an act of worship and a practical expression of the transformative power of the gospel.

The Heart of Simple Giving: Trust and Surrender

Earlier, I mentioned a church member named John. Though he didn't flaunt his generosity, I couldn't help but notice it. He was generous to our church, and he was generous to those in need in the church and beyond.

I asked him a basic question one time: "John, how did you develop a life of generosity?"

He, of course, was reluctant to respond because he didn't want the focus to be on him. I don't remember his precise words, but they were something like "If we can't trust God to provide for us financially and to give abundantly, we can't really trust him at all."

Our money is often the last thing we are willing to release

as we seek to follow God in our local church. But in many ways it is the beginning of truly trusting him.

At the center of simple giving lies a radical trust in God's provision. When we decide to give generously, we are essentially declaring that God is our ultimate provider. This act of trust is not always easy, especially in a culture that emphasizes financial security and self-reliance. Yet the Bible is clear: Our security does not come from our bank accounts, but from our relationship with the Creator of all things.

In Luke 12:22-34, Jesus speaks directly to this point. He encourages his followers not to worry about their lives, what they will eat, or what they will wear. Instead, he points to the birds of the air and the lilies of the field as examples of God's care. "If God cares so wonderfully for flowers that are here today and thrown into the fire tomorrow, he will certainly care for you. Why do you have so little faith?"

Again, read his words closely. If we are not generous and simple givers, we are telling God we do not trust him. We have little faith.

Simple giving also requires a surrender of control—a willingness to let go of the need to manage every aspect of our lives. This surrender is not an act of recklessness but a demonstration of faith. It acknowledges that God is in control, and he knows what we need even before we ask. As we give generously, we become partners in God's work on earth, co-laborers in his Kingdom.

Practical Implications of Simple Giving

The call to simple giving has profound implications for how we live our daily lives. It challenges us to examine our priorities and to reframe our understanding of wealth and success. Here are some practical ways to embody simple giving:

1. Prioritize God's Kingdom over Material Wealth

Simple giving means putting the Kingdom of God above all other pursuits. It invites us to reallocate our resources—time, money, and energy—toward initiatives that further God's mission. This might involve supporting church ministries, local charities, or global missions that spread the gospel. It is a reminder that our true treasure is found in heaven, and with our earthly possessions we are merely stewards of God's bounty.

2. Cultivate a Generous Heart

Generosity begins in the heart. A spirit of simple giving is cultivated through prayer, in Scripture, and through a conscious commitment to live out the teachings of Jesus. As we immerse ourselves in the Word, our perspectives shift; we begin to see that every act of giving is a reflection of God's unconditional love for us. This transformation starts with gratitude—recognizing that every gift we have is a blessing from God—and moves toward an attitude of abundance rather than scarcity.

3. Embrace Sacrificial Giving

Sacrificial giving is at the heart of simple generosity. It's not about the size of the gift, but the willingness to sacrifice personal comfort for the sake of others. This could mean donating beyond what is comfortable, investing in causes that challenge us, or even giving of our time and talents in ways that might not be immediately gratifying. The widow's offering, for example, reminds us that the value of a gift is not measured by its monetary amount but by the sacrifice behind it.

4. Integrate Generosity into Every Aspect of Life

Simple giving should not be compartmentalized—it must permeate every area of our lives. Whether it's offering a listening ear, volunteering at a local shelter, or simply sharing words of encouragement, every act of kindness is a form of giving. By integrating generosity into our daily routines, we create a lifestyle that reflects the heart of Christ. Our homes, workplaces, and communities become arenas for the transformative power of giving, turning everyday interactions into opportunities to display God's love.

5. Trust God's Provision

One of the greatest challenges in practicing simple giving is overcoming the fear of lack. Yet, when we trust in God's provision, we are freed from the anxiety of scarcity. Jesus' teaching in the Sermon on the Mount reminds us that God cares for the birds and the lilies, and so much more for us. Simple giving is an act of faith—a declaration that God will provide for our needs even as we step out in obedience. As we experience God's faithfulness, our trust deepens, and our capacity to give expands.

The Impact of Simple Giving on the Community

The ripple effects of simple giving extend far beyond the individual believer. When we choose to live generously, we become catalysts for change in our communities. Simple giving fosters a spirit of unity and solidarity, bridging divides and building relationships rooted in mutual care and compassion. Churches and communities that embrace simple generosity often become beacons of hope, demonstrating that love and service are powerful antidotes to the divisiveness and materialism of contemporary culture.

Moreover, simple giving challenges societal norms by redefining success and wealth. In a world that often measures success by financial accumulation and social status, the radical disciple offers an alternative model—one in which value is determined by love, sacrifice, and the willingness to serve others. This countercultural stance has the power to inspire others to reevaluate their own lives, sparking a movement of generosity that can transform not only individuals but entire communities.

Overcoming Barriers to Radical Giving

Despite its beauty and biblical mandate, simple giving is not without its challenges. Several barriers can hinder our willingness to give generously.

Fear of Financial Insecurity

Many people are hesitant to give because they fear not having enough for their own needs. The uncertainty of life and the pressures of modern financial demands can create a mindset of scarcity. However, the Bible calls us to trust in God's provision. By shifting our focus from what we lack to what we have been graciously given, we begin to see that true wealth is not in our bank accounts but in our relationship with God.

Cultural and Societal Influences

Living in a consumer-driven society, it is easy to become ensnared by messages that equate success with material wealth. Simple giving requires us to counter these messages with a gospel-centered vision—a life marked by selflessness and the desire to serve rather than accumulate. This shift often involves redefining our understanding of success and finding contentment in Christ rather than in possessions.

Personal Pride and Attachment

Our attachment to our belongings and our sense of control can be significant obstacles to simple giving. The act of giving requires humility and the recognition that every possession is a gift from God. Letting go of this attachment can be difficult, but it is essential for embracing a lifestyle of generosity. When we acknowledge that all we have is held in trust by God, we free ourselves from the bondage of materialism and open our hearts to a deeper, more fulfilling way of living.

Problems with the Recipients of Simple Giving

There have been a few occasions when Nellie Jo and I have been disappointed in how recipients of gifts from us responded. For example, we made a major gift to a person in the community who was struggling to make basic ends meet. Our hope was that she would take care of her barely functioning car, get a sufficient amount of food, find a decent place to rent, and pay pressing bills.

Much to my chagrin, she wasted the money. Let me state it more honestly: I resented how she responded with this new amount of cash she had. Nellie Jo politely chastised me. She reminded me that, when we give, we let go of the funds. Our role is to be obedient to God's call for us to live a life of simple giving. Our role is not to be the bookkeeper and administrator of the funds we give away.

Such a problem can be common in churches. We don't like how the funds are expended in our church, so we withhold or designate our giving to meet our preferences. That is not simple giving; that is control-based giving. Unless the church demonstrates gross malfeasance of funds, we are called to give and let go.

That is simple giving.

Living Out Simple Giving Today

Simple giving is not an abstract ideal—it is a practical, daily commitment to follow Jesus. It is a lifestyle that begins with a personal decision to live for God and extends outward, impacting our families, communities, and even the broader world. Here are some actionable steps to integrate simple giving into your life.

1. *Prayer and reflection.* Start each day with a prayer of gratitude and surrender. Ask God to help you see your resources as his and to guide you in using them for his purposes.
2. *Budgeting with purpose.* Review your finances and set aside a portion for ministry, charity, or community projects. Treat this as an investment in the Kingdom of God rather than a sacrifice.
3. *Intentional acts of kindness.* Look for opportunities to give—whether it's donating to a local food bank, offering your time to help a neighbor, or supporting a church initiative.
4. *Sharing your testimony.* Reflect on how simple giving has transformed your own life and be open

to sharing these experiences with others. Your story might inspire someone else to take a step of faith.

5. *Community engagement.* Join or start a group dedicated to supporting local outreach programs. Collective giving can multiply the impact of individual contributions, creating a network of love and support.

The Crucial Commitment of Giving in Our Church

Jesus' life was the ultimate example of simple giving. He gave himself completely for the sake of humanity—living a life marked by service, compassion, and self-sacrifice. His teachings challenge us to move beyond a transactional view of giving and to embrace a transformative, radical generosity that touches every aspect of our lives. This is not a call to reckless abandonment of our responsibilities, but rather a call to trust deeply in God's provision and to live in a way that reflects his boundless love.

While our generosity and simple giving should extend beyond our local church, it should also begin with our local church. My personal conviction is that I will not give less than ten percent of my gross income to my local church. I can and do give more, and I can and do give to other causes.

Jesus did not teach on money for money's sake. Though the four Gospels are replete with such teachings, including eleven parables, Jesus taught far more than Personal Finance 101.

Indeed, if there is a common theme in his teachings on money, it is simple. The money God has entrusted to us is to be used for his glory. If we have any hesitation to do exactly what he wants us to with that money, we can't be trusted to do anything else.

The story of the rich young ruler (Matthew 19:16-22) is instructive in many ways. The young man was morally upright. He obeyed all the legal commandments. But Jesus was unflinchingly blunt with him. The Savior told the young man that God could not use him unless he gave away all of his possessions to the poor.

The scene unfolds like this in Matthew 19:21-22: "Jesus told him, 'If you want to be perfect, go and sell all your possessions and give the money to the poor, and you will have treasure in heaven. Then come, follow me.' But when the young man heard this, he went away sad, for he had many possessions."

Money and possessions were the young man's idols. Unless he was truly willing to let go of all of them, he could not follow Jesus.

The rich young man was asked to make a crucial commitment. He was unwilling to do so.

Simple giving is not just another ministry in the church. It is the area of our lives that must demonstrate total commitment. You might not be asked to sell everything you have and give it away. But you might.

It can be the crucial commitment that makes us or breaks us toward following Christ.

It is the crucial commitment we must make as a member of the body of Christ.

It's just that important.

Three Questions

1. What reasons have caused you to hold back from simple giving? How have you responded?
2. Because we are saved by grace and not works, what does the story of the young rich man tell us about following Christ?
3. Why should the local church be our first point and place of giving?

9

Reaching Out

I love church consultations.

From the time I did my first consultation in 1988, and through every one I have done since then, I am thankful to God for the opportunities he has given me.

I get to work with churches of all sizes, denominations, nondenominations, and locations. I get to see the local body of Christ up close and personal. I get to listen and learn.

After hundreds and hundreds of consultations, I can say unequivocally that I have learned a lot. Every congregation has its unique features. Every congregation has a personality all its own.

Sadly, though, most congregations have a commonality. They are not evangelistic.

It usually takes a consultation for members to realize that evangelism is missing in their lives and in the ministries of the church. We provide churches a thorough self-examination tool called Know Your Church. Guess which area of ministry is typically considered the weakest in the church?

Yes, evangelism is the self-described weakest ministry in churches in 94 percent of our surveys.

Churches know something is wrong. The members understand that evangelism is lacking. Why, then, don't they do something about it?

Simply stated, it is the crucial commitment that has not been made.

A local church is not truly a church unless it is reaching people with the gospel. Without sharing the message of Christ, a congregation may function as a community, but it fails to fulfill its primary purpose.

Evangelism—obedience to Christ's command to reach the lost—is the lifeblood of the church. When a church becomes inwardly focused, it risks becoming a comfortable gathering without impact. Let's explore the crucial commitment of sharing the gospel, examining how evangelism flows from obedient church life.

A Last Will and Testament

My wife and I had our lawyer write a new will for us a few years ago. Life situations had changed. All the sons were out of the house and married with children of their own. We needed an updated will.

Though our attorney made several changes in the will for our consideration, one key aspect did not change. We wanted most of our assets to go to our sons and their families. We did not simply desire to give them all of our earthly belongings, we wanted to make a clear statement of our love for them. We wanted our final words to say clearly to them, "We love you."

Jesus' final words on earth, recorded in Acts 1:8, serve as his last will and testament to his disciples. He said, "You will receive power when the Holy Spirit comes upon you. And you will be my witnesses, telling people about me everywhere—in Jerusalem, throughout Judea, in Samaria, and to the ends of the earth." These words are not just a promise of empowerment—they are a command. The church is called not only to gather for worship and fellowship but also to go out and share the good news of salvation.

This mandate is the foundation of true church life. It reminds us that the purpose of the church is to evangelize and make disciples. Just as a last will and testament conveys a final, irrevocable desire, Jesus' words were meant to set in motion a movement that would transform the world. They are the definitive instructions for what a local church must become—a sending body that reaches beyond its walls.

Jesus' commission reveals that every believer is expected to participate in evangelism. His words cut to the core: The church exists to witness to the gospel. If a church remains closed off from its community, if it clings only to its internal comforts, then it is failing to live out the command of its Savior. Evangelism is not a side activity; it is the final charge of every disciple, meant to be practiced through the local church.

Evangelism is a crucial commitment.

Not Everything Is Evangelism

Many churches boast of strong community ministries and social services. They organize food drives, support local charities, and engage in outreach to meet practical needs. These are commendable and essential expressions of love. However, many of these activities do not have an explicit evangelistic goal. They serve the community, but without intentionally sharing the gospel, the impact remains incomplete.

Our team at Church Answers has worked with countless churches that have incredible community ministries. In many cases, though, these churches see their ministries as the key outreach of the church.

We recently worked with a church in North Carolina that has a great community ministry. It includes an annual event of fun, games, and food with the goal to raise more funds for the ministry. They told us more than 1,500 people have attended for each of the past seventeen years. That means the church has had more than 25,000 opportunities to minister to people in the community.

How many of those community members has this church reached with the gospel?

Exactly zero.

Evangelism is not present at all.

When a church's focus shifts solely to meeting material needs without proclaiming the message of salvation, it risks missing the point of the gospel. Good works should flow from a heart transformed by Christ, not serve as an end in themselves. The New Testament makes it clear that evangelism is a distinct responsibility. It is possible to do wonderful ministry while neglecting the explicit call to tell others about Jesus. That is why the local church must balance its practical outreach with a bold, intentional witness to the gospel message.

The challenge is to ensure that every act of service also points people to Christ. Whether you are distributing food or running a community event, the purpose should be evangelistic—to create opportunities to share the hope found in Jesus. Church members must be equipped to see evangelism woven into every activity rather than treating it as a separate, optional ministry.

To be clear, though, evangelism must ultimately become a crucial commitment of each member. It is certainly good to have evangelistic ministries and programs. But those ministries should be replete with members who have made a crucial commitment to share the gospel themselves.

The Local Church as the Path of Discipleship

The New Testament consistently emphasizes the local church as the means by which new believers are discipled. Discipleship is not a solitary pursuit; it occurs best in community. The early church met regularly for teaching, fellowship, and prayer (Acts 2:42-47). In those gatherings, new believers were nurtured, equipped, and sent out as witnesses to the world.

Discipleship and evangelism are inextricably linked. When people become disciples, they are called to learn and grow within the context of the local church. It is there they encounter the transforming power of the gospel, receive teaching from mature believers, and are challenged to live out their faith. The local church is, therefore, the natural launching pad for evangelism. As disciples mature in their faith, they are equipped to share the gospel with others.

This process is outlined throughout the New Testament. Paul, for example, spent his ministry writing letters to local congregations, instructing them on how to live as disciples of Christ. The church is not a collection of isolated individuals; it is a community where every member is accountable to one another and empowered by the Holy Spirit to reach the lost.

Four Big Barriers to Sharing the Gospel

Even with the clear mandate of Acts 1:8 and the strong discipleship model of the early church, many believers struggle with evangelism. Four common barriers frequently hinder the sharing of the gospel: busyness, apathy, fear, and lack of self-discipline.

Busyness

In today's fast-paced world, schedules are packed and priorities are many. Often, Christians find it difficult to carve out time for intentional evangelism. When every day is filled with work, family obligations, and other responsibilities, sharing the gospel often gets pushed to the back burner. Yet, if we commit to our local church and make time for fellowship and outreach, we find that evangelism is not an extra burden but a natural outflow of our daily lives.

Indeed, many church members tell us they are too busy to stay involved in their local church. Frankly, a number of pastors have communicated that same reality to us.

Josh, for example, is a pastor in Florida. He said, "Everybody's busy, including church members. Florida has so many places people can enjoy for free or for a nominal price. Between their busyness with their families, their work, their sports, and Florida fun, we have to expect that their commitment to our church is not high. Do you understand?"

No, I don't understand.

We make time for those things that are important to us. If you truly believed the biblical teachings about the importance of the local church, you would have time for it. If you truly believed the urgency of the Great Commission and sharing the gospel, you would make time for them. Among the five crucial commitments, the commitment to be used of God in evangelism through your local church is the first to wane. The other crucial commitments will follow the example of the commitment of evangelism.

Apathy

Satan will do everything in his limited power to stop us from sharing the gospel. He moves church members to complacency, where they become desensitized to the urgency of the gospel. They may be comfortable in their routines and reluctant to step out of their comfort zone. Apathy can manifest as indifference to the needs of those who have not yet heard the gospel. This complacency undermines the church's mission and stifles the potential for transformation.

I was talking to my teenage grandson about evangelism. He has read some of my writings on evangelism, and we've had several discussions about it. His question both intrigued me and convicted me. "If," he began, "we really believe that Jesus is the only way of salvation, why is evangelism not a fire drill in our churches?" He used "fire drill" as a double entendre.

Above all, his question convicted me. Why is evangelism not a fire drill consistently in my own life? Why is it not a crucial commitment for me consistently in the church where God has placed me?

Those are not rhetorical questions. They are questions I must answer honestly to God. If I don't share my faith, I am essentially telling the world that I couldn't care less if they go to heaven.

Apathy, indeed, might be one of the most potent tools of the enemy.

Fear

Fear of rejection, fear of failure, and even fear of offending others are common obstacles. Sharing the gospel can be intimidating, especially when we worry about the responses we might receive. However, the promise of the Holy Spirit empowers us to overcome these fears. Remember, our mandate comes directly from Christ, and he has equipped us to be his witnesses.

When our team conducted a research project on the unchurched several years ago, we found that only five percent of respondents were antagonistic to someone sharing the gospel with them. Most non-Christians welcomed a conversation about eternal matters. Our fears of rejection and offending someone are mostly unfounded.

So what if someone is offended by Christ's offer of salvation? So what if they express disdain for our "religion"? It is a small price to pay compared to someone hearing the gospel and responding positively to the message.

My grandson's question was spot-on. Evangelism should

be a fire drill for each of us personally, and for our churches corporately.

Lack of Self-Discipline

Evangelism requires consistency and intentionality. Without a disciplined approach, it's easy to let opportunities slip by. Many believers struggle to maintain a regular pattern of prayer, relationship building, and sharing their faith. Developing self-discipline is essential to overcoming this barrier and ensuring that evangelism becomes a habitual part of our lives.

Recognizing these barriers is the first step toward overcoming them. By intentionally addressing busyness, combating apathy, confronting our fears, and cultivating self-discipline, we can transform our witness and make evangelism a natural extension of our daily walk with Christ.

We can make it a crucial commitment.

When Evangelism Is a Crucial Commitment

When evangelism is embraced as a crucial commitment, it reshapes not only the individual believer but the entire church as well. This commitment calls us to a higher standard of obedience—a standard exemplified by programs such as the Hope Initiative. This thirty-day program challenges church members to commit to an evangelistic lifestyle, stepping out in faith to share the gospel with those around them. The program, which uses principles from my book

Pray & Go, has transformed many congregations by creating a culture of proactive evangelism.

A church that prioritizes evangelism as a crucial commitment understands that its very survival depends on reaching out. The local church is not a social club; it is the body of Christ sent out to make disciples. When every member commits to sharing the gospel, the impact is exponential. Lives are transformed, communities are renewed, and the Kingdom of God advances.

Embracing evangelism as a crucial commitment means integrating it into every facet of church life. It means that even community programs and outreach events are designed with an evangelistic purpose in mind. It means that every service, every small group, and every ministry becomes an opportunity to share the good news of Jesus Christ.

As you consider your own life and the life of your church, ask yourself: *Is evangelism woven into the fabric of my community? Are my fellow believers and I actively sharing the gospel, or have we become inwardly focused?* A church that neglects evangelism is a church that is on a certain path toward death.

This commitment to evangelism is not optional. It is a mandate from Christ, a final command that shapes every aspect of what it means to be his disciples. When evangelism is a crucial commitment, every act of service, every conversation, and every interaction becomes a chance to witness to the transforming power of the gospel.

The journey toward a life of significance is not one of isolation, but of connection and obedience within the local church. As you embrace simple giving, radical prayer, and faithful attendance, let your commitment extend to sharing the gospel. In doing so, you fulfill the Great Commission and become an instrument through which God changes the world.

When we commit to evangelism in our everyday lives—through consistent outreach, disciple-making, and sacrificial service—we become the hands and feet of Jesus in a hurting world.

May you be challenged to view evangelism not as an optional extra, but as an essential, life-giving component of your walk with Christ. Embrace the call, overcome the barriers, and step into the mission with bold, unwavering faith.

Please hear me clearly. The crucial commitment of evangelism cannot and should not be taken lightly. It is spiritual warfare. The enemy will fight us fiercely.

From my four decades of working with churches, I can see the clear strategy and tactics of Satan to hinder our work of evangelism. He wants us to forget about it. He wants you to read these words and move on quickly to something else.

Apathy is the most potent weapon the enemy has. When we move on to something else, when we forget about the priority of evangelism, and when we fail to see the eternal urgency of sharing the gospel, Satan has won the battle.

So, I am pleading with you as I ask the question, "Are you ready to make this crucial commitment?" Frankly, you can forget the other four if you move on without making this commitment.

Are you willing to ask God right now to empower you to fulfill this commitment? Are you willing to ask God to remind you daily about this commitment? Are you really ready?

It is a most crucial commitment.

Three Questions

1. How does a local church's commitment to evangelism impact its overall mission and discipleship?

2. In what ways can overcoming barriers like busyness, apathy, fear, and lack of self-discipline transform our approach to sharing the gospel?

3. How can programs like the Hope Initiative and a book such as *Pray & Go* help cultivate a culture of evangelism in your church?

10

The Commitment That Changes Everything

I certainly remember December 17, 1977. It was my wedding day. Nellie Jo and I surprised no one with our intention to marry. We had dated for more than five years. Thom-and-Nellie-Jo was almost one word to our family and peers.

But I had no idea what was to come.

The birth of three incredible sons who bring me greater joy every single day. Meeting my future daughters-in-law and marveling how God brought these gifts to my sons. The births of ten grandchildren and the adoption of an eleventh.

Shedding tears when my sons embraced Christ as the Savior of their lives. Doing the same with my grandchildren. Officiating my sons' weddings (with enduring apologies to one daughter-in-law for saying her name wrong during the vows).

Writing books, lots of books. Serving as a pastor of four churches and as interim pastor of nine more. Becoming dean of a seminary. Becoming president of one of the largest Christian resource companies in the world. Founding a church consulting and resource company.

There have been even more blessings. Hundreds more. So many blessings.

But that date in 1977 was also the starting point for a lot of pain.

The death of my parents—both suddenly. The death of a grandchild. Nearly losing Nellie Jo to cancer. Her multiple surgeries, chemotherapy, radiation treatment. Feeling helpless as she was so terribly sick. The death of Nellie Jo's dad.

Feeling helpless again as two sons were fired as pastors of their churches for no good reason. My own vocational challenges, critics, and doubts.

So how have Nellie Jo and I made it almost to the half-century point in our marriage?

I promise you, it has not always been easy. Marriage has revealed many of my deep flaws—flaws that could destroy a marriage. Anger. Jealously. Impatience. Neglect. Narcissism. Workaholism.

There but for the grace of God go I . . .

At times, only one thing has held our marriage together: the commitment we both made before God and others that we would be together until death do us part.

We are still married—yes, because we love each other, but also because we made commitments. Commitments to each other. Commitments to God and before God. Commitments in the presence of family and friends.

We are still married because we committed to stay married.

It was a commitment that changed everything.

Commitment to Your Church

Sure, there are reasons to leave a church, but not many biblically legitimate ones.

I was speaking to a fellow church member recently, and he told me that he was at our church because he had to leave another church.

I don't know if he could read my face, but I was feeling a cringe factor. *Here we go again, another church hopper who didn't get his way, so he ran to the next imperfect church.*

I was wrong.

He shared with me the false doctrine that was being taught at his church—including salvation other than through Christ alone. He'd gone to the pastor. He'd gone to the elders. It was all to no avail. So he left the church. Yes, his reason was legitimate.

I met a lady at conference, a widow who had recently left her church for another one in town. Her situation was challenging. She changed churches because she wanted to be near her mother, who had just been placed in a memory care center. The ravages of Alzheimer's had already taken a serious toll. And though the two churches were technically in the same city, the drive from one church to the other took forty minutes.

She left her church for a good reason.

But when a church member moves from one church to another in the same community, it is typically for the wrong reason. Someone hurt their feelings. They didn't like the music. The sermons were too long or too boring. Many pastors hear these cringe words at some point: "I am just not getting fed."

Please don't take church membership lightly. Please don't think of worship attendance, small group involvement, and giving as just a checklist of ways for you to prove your religiosity. Your commitment to your church is critical. It is likely one of the most important commitments you can make.

Let's reflect on a few biblical realities.

The Church Is Analogous to a Committed Marriage

I know we covered this point earlier, but we've got to grasp the seriousness of it. It is not incidental that Christ called the church his bride, and he is the bridegroom. Of course, Christ is the perfectly committed party, but we should demonstrate our commitment to him as well.

It would be difficult to discern a specific point in our cultural history when church commitment became lackadaisical or nonexistent. I can remember when I would feel disobedient if I was at church only two weeks a month. In many churches today, we call half-committed church members "elders." I write that with humor—but not totally.

Like the metaphorical frog in the kettle, we have not noticed the changes because they have been incremental. But the commitment of many church members today is sorely lacking.

As a reminder, here are ten reasons we should be committed to our local church. These ten are only a starting point. I encourage you to take time to look up each of the biblical passages.

Ten Reasons to Be Committed to Your Church

1. Biblical Obedience (Hebrews 10:24-25)

Scripture explicitly instructs believers not to forsake assembling together. Regular attendance and involvement in a local church is obedience to God's clear command. A "50 percent–attendance Christian" is a disobedient Christian.

2. Mutual Encouragement and Spiritual Growth (Ephesians 4:11-16)

The local church is the primary place designed by God for believers to grow spiritually, build each other up, and mature together in faith and character. We were not meant to "go to church alone." We need each other.

3. Exercise Your Spiritual Gifts (1 Corinthians 12:4-7)

Every believer is uniquely gifted by the Holy Spirit for service. A commitment to a local church provides the context for these gifts to be identified, developed, and utilized effectively. Remember, when Paul addressed the issue of spiritual gifts, he did so only in the context of a local body of believers. The local body of Christ needs all members functioning for the greater good of all.

4. Community and Fellowship (Acts 2:42-47)

God created us for community. The local church provides the God-ordained environment where believers experience authentic, meaningful relationships that reflect God's love and unity. This will become even more important with Gen Z and Gen Alpha. These younger generations have become relationship-hindered by their addiction to and dependence on the digital world, particularly with smartphones and social media.

5. Accountability and Discipleship (Proverbs 27:17; Galatians 6:1-2)

Spiritual growth thrives in an environment of accountability. Committing to a local church helps believers guard against drifting spiritually and provides accountability for personal holiness. Accountability should be a joy, not a burden.

6. Fulfillment of the Great Commission (Matthew 28:18-20; Acts 1:8)

The local church is the vehicle through which Christ intends to accomplish the Great Commission. Through collective efforts, believers participate in reaching their local community and the world with the gospel. Sadly, most churches today practice the Great Omission instead of the Great Commission.

7. Support in Times of Need (Galatians 6:10; James 5:13-16)

The local church provides practical care, support, and encouragement in times of difficulty, grief, or crisis, fulfilling the biblical command to bear one another's burdens. I continue to be amazed how the local church comes together for those in need. Of course, the members of the local church must be present to care for others.

8. Submission to Spiritual Leadership (Hebrews 13:17)

God establishes spiritual leaders within the local church who shepherd and guide believers. Committing to a local church places believers under godly leadership, ensuring doctrinal soundness and pastoral care. *Submission* is not a negative word. It is liberating to know that others are not only looking over us, but they are also looking out for us.

9. Corporate Worship (Psalm 95:1-6; Colossians 3:16)

Gathering regularly with fellow believers in worship aligns our hearts collectively toward God, reminding us of his sovereignty, grace, and goodness. When God's people worship together, we get a marvelous preview of the joy we will have together in heaven.

10. Visible Witness to the World (John 13:34-35)

The church's unity, love, and commitment to each other serve as a visible testimony to an unbelieving world. This witness has a powerful evangelistic impact. It has been ironic to read non-Christians advocating for churches. Jonathan Haidt has been one such voice in recent years with his book *The Anxious Generation*, but many other secular voices are echoing the same theme. Our culture feels the void of churches that no longer are vibrant witnesses to the world. Again, ironically, our culture wants the local church back.

God's Plan for Your Life

Think about it. The birth of the local church is recorded in the book of Acts. From Acts 2 to Revelation 3, the New Testament focuses on the local church. Those books account for a large swath of the New Testament. The local church is vitally important to God; the local church should be important to us as well.

Do you want to make a difference in this world in the

brief years God has given you? Do you want to have a true purpose on this planet?

According to the authority of God's Word, you will make a difference if you do so as a committed church member. That is God's plan for your life. That is how you can make a difference. That is how you can be a part of a movement that is turning the world upside down.

The local church is not just another organization. The local church is not a social club. The local church is not just a civic society.

The local church is God's plan for your life to make a difference in this world. Such is the reason you have been challenged to make at least five crucial commitments. For sure, there are more than five commitments you could make, but the five we have focused on in these pages are sufficient to move you toward becoming the type of church member God intended.

Revolution

If you know anything about me, you know I love my family. I talk and write about my wife, my sons, my daughters-in-law, and my grandchildren incessantly. I am sure some people have rolled their eyes as I speak about my family members. *There he goes again*, they likely think.

I often tell people that my sons are also my best friends. It is absolutely true. I have adored them from their births to the middle-aged men they are today. Sam. Art. Jess. Just writing their names fills me with joy, love, and pride.

That is why a story like one by Randy Loubier in *Christianity Today* brought me to tears. Randy hated church people. In fact, his first-person article says it in the title, "I Hated 'Church People.' But I Knew I Needed Them."[6] His story is a tragedy. He had been fired from his job because he was a whistleblower. Then, in less than three weeks, both of his sons lost their girlfriends, one to suicide, the other to an automobile crash.

I have walked with my sons through tough times. My middle son lost his good friend in an automobile accident. As I noted earlier, two of my sons were fired from churches. My youngest son lost his child, Will, just one hour after birth.

I think I cry the biggest tears when my own child is hurting.

No, it is not hard for me to imagine the pain Randy Loubier, his wife, and their sons were experiencing. I hurt just reading his story.

At both funerals, a lady named Debbie reached out to the Loubier family. At the second funeral, the mother of the deceased girlfriend expressed her concern for the son who had lost his girlfriend. Randy knew she was a churchgoing Christian, but he was taken aback when she provided consolation in the midst of her own deep grief.

Randy's words reflect well his surprise: *"What is going on here? She just lost her daughter, her best friend, and she wants to care for my son? Who does that?*"[7]

It took only a few minutes on the ride home before Randy's wife said, "I'm going to start going to church." I love Randy's response. It reminds me of something similar that happened to me. He responded factually: "It was not a request or an invitation to join her. She knew I hated church. Still, I volunteered to come along."[8]

Yep, I have volunteered for my wife on a few occasions.

Randy's father-in-law sent him a Bible. Though he had sworn he would never read that book, he made the decision to read it from cover to cover. By the time he finished the Old Testament he had fallen in love with the written Word. By the time he got to the Gospel of John, he fell in love with the living Word.

Randy became a believer in Christ.

His is only one of the millions and millions of stories of believers who have revolutionized the world through their local churches.

Yes, it is nothing less than a revolution.

But lest we forget where this part of Randy's story began, he reminds us.

"Make no mistake, the church first sparked my curiosity. If God's people hadn't made me wonder about their peculiar love, I never would have cracked open God's Word, and I never would have fallen in love myself."[9]

It is time. It is time we join the revolution, a revolution that began with a ragtag group of believers in Jerusalem. A revolution that has changed the world. A revolution that quickly caught the eyes and the hearts of onlookers as the early church "enjoy[ed] the goodwill of all the people" (Acts 2:47). The consequence was people getting saved every day.

You are not called to go to a church just to go through the motions. You are called to be a part of a church that will get the gospel witness in motion. Living your life to the fullest as a committed church member is one of your highest callings.

The End

I was a twenty-four-year-old businessman, unchurched and hungry for something more. When my wife was pregnant with our first child, she gently nudged me to consider going to church. Her gentle persuasion and my impending fatherhood were all I needed.

We found a church.

We became part of a revolution.

That was the beginning.

But now the end is near. I do not know how many years I have left, but common mortality tables remind me that time is running out.

My life was renewed in a church. My purpose was rekindled in a church. And my path was remade in a church.

I became a part of a revolution, but the revolution also became a part of me.

Sure, I have some regrets. And for certain, I have blown it on many occasions. But there are some regrets I will never have. I will never regret my marriage. I will never regret being a father. I will never regret saying *yes* to Jesus. And I will never regret being a part of the churches I have loved and served.

That is why, in the sum of it all, I have not lived a regretful life. I might be nearing the end, but it has been an incredible journey.

Five Crucial Commitments

In some ways, my life's journey has been one of reminding people of the beautiful bride of Christ in the local church. She is not perfect. She has her human flaws. She makes mistakes. But she is the bride of Christ.

Love her. Embrace her. Cherish her.

And if you're married, remember the vows you made to your spouse. Let them be a reminder that you should make vows to the bride of Christ, your local church. And even when you slip or fail, you will return to these vows.

Throughout this book, I have focused on five specific areas for greater commitment to your church. We call them Crucial Commitments.

1. *I commit to pray for my church.* I am not committing to perfunctory prayer; I am committing to radical prayer. I pray that the gospel will turn our church upside down. I will pray for our pastor and for the sermons each week. I pray that we will be a church that changes the world.
2. *I commit to attend my church.* This commitment means that I will strive every week to show up, that my church will not be just another activity on my busy list. I will make faithful attendance every single week one of my highest priorities.
3. *I commit to be a part of a group in my church.* It is in small groups that true community takes place. It is the place where accountability is healthy and present. I will care for my fellow group members, and I will invite others to be a part of our community.
4. *I commit to be a simple giver to my church.* That means I give simply and abundantly. That means I give simply and joyfully. That means I give simply with no strings attached. That means that I will trust God to provide as I give simply.
5. *I commit to be a gospel witness through my church.* God gave me the gift of salvation through his Son Jesus Christ. I am honored to tell others about Jesus. I will invite people to church. I will pray for opportunities to share the good news of Christ.

We have the incredible opportunity to fulfill the purpose God has given us: to glorify him as we serve him through the local church. We make these commitments as a starting point. We know that our simple acts of commitment can change the world. And they can certainly give purpose and meaning to our lives.

These are crucial commitments.

Read them.

Repeat them.

Commit to them.

And see what God will do through you.

Three Questions

1. What are the five commitments articulated throughout this book?
2. How do you move from *making* the commitments to *living* the commitments?
3. Why is faithful weekly attendance at your church so vitally important?

Notes

1. Ying Chen and Tyler J. VanderWeele, "Associations of Religious Upbringing with Subsequent Health and Well-Being from Adolescence to Young Adulthood: An Outcome-Wide Analysis," *American Journal of Epidemiology* 187, no. 11 (November 2018): 2355–2364, https://doi.org/10.1093/aje/kwy142. This research examined the impact of religious involvement during adolescence on various health and well-being outcomes in young adulthood, particularly focusing on practices such as attending weekly religious services. The study found that individuals who attended religious services at least weekly during their youth reported greater life satisfaction and positivity in their twenties. They were also less likely to experience depressive symptoms, smoke, use illicit drugs, or have a sexually transmitted infection, compared to those with less frequent or no religious involvement.
2. Ying Chen, quoted in "Religious Upbringing Linked to Better Health and Well-Being During Early Adulthood," Harvard T. H. Chan School of Public Health press release, September 13, 2008, https://hsph.harvard.edu/news/religious-upbringing-adult-health.
3. J. Maureen Henderson, "Working on the Weekend Is the New Normal and That's a Bad Thing," *Forbes*, April 28, 2017, https://www.forbes.com/sites/jmaureenhenderson/2017/04/28/working-on-the-weekend-is-the-new-normal-and-thats-a-bad-thing.

4. Elaine Pofeldt, "Survey: Nearly 30% of Americans Are Self-Employed," *Forbes*, May 30, 2020, https://www.forbes.com/sites/elainepofeldt/2020/05/30/survey-nearly-30-of-americans-are-self-employed.
5. US Religion Census, "US Religion Census Shows Both Stability and Change in Congregational Life," Press Release 2020, https://www.usreligioncensus.org/node/1641.
6. Randy Loubier, "I Hated Church People. But I Knew I Needed Them.," *Christianity Today*, March 2024, https://www.christianitytoday.com/2024/02/randy-loubier-testimony-hated-church-people-funerals.
7. Loubier, "I Hated Church People."
8. Loubier, "I Hated Church People."
9. Loubier, "I Hated Church People."

About the Author

Thom S. Rainer is founder and CEO of Church Answers. With forty years of ministry experience, Thom has spent a lifetime committed to the growth and health of the local church and its leaders. Prior to founding Church Answers, he served as president and CEO of LifeWay Christian Resources. Before LifeWay, he served for twelve years at The Southern Baptist Theological Seminary, where he was the founding dean of the Billy Graham School of Missions, Evangelism, and Ministry. He is a 1977 graduate of the University of Alabama and earned his MDiv and PhD from The Southern Baptist Theological Seminary. In addition to speaking in hundreds of venues over the past thirty years, Thom led the Rainer Group, a church and denominational consulting firm that provided church health insights to more than five hundred churches and other organizations from 1990 to 2005. Thom is the author of more than forty books. He and his wife, Nellie Jo, live in Franklin, Tennessee.